THE SISTERS ARE ASKING

Winfrid Herbst, S.D.S.

THE NEWMAN PRESS
Westminster • Maryland • 1957

THE SISTERS ARE ASKING

Imprimi potest: Paul Schuster, S.D.S.
                     Provincial

Nihil obstat: Edward A. Cerny, S.S., D.D.
                     Censor Librorum

Imprimatur: ✠ Francis P. Keough, D.D.
                     Archbishop of Baltimore
                     May 18, 1956

Second Printing, 1957

Copyright © 1956, by the Newman Press
Library of Congress Catalog Card Number: 56-9383
Manufactured in the United States of America
by H. Wolff, New York

FOREWORD

Once upon a time in my missionary career, I made it a practice, even in retreats to Sisters, to have a question box into which the retreatants could place their questions, to be answered by me in the so-called question-box conferences near the end of the retreat.

In the following pages a number of such questions are answered, in all the interesting and provocative disorder in which they were spilled out of the question box and picked up at random for reply.

I hope they will be read as avidly as they were listened to in those days when we went "apart into a desert place to rest awhile" in the Lord.

W. H., S.D.S

CONTENTS

STRIVING AFTER PERFECTION

What, in your opinion, should be some of the characteristics of the ideal Sister?

Every Sister, of course, should be truly Christlike, Marylike, our Lady's double, as becomes a spouse of the Divine Savior. St. Clement Mary Hofbauer once said to the Visitandines of Vienna: "When I pass in front of your monastery, I lift my hat twice: first to salute our Lord dwelling in the Blessed Sacrament in the midst of you, His spouses, and then to salute you, who are His faithful spouses."

But, to go somewhat into detail, let us say that a Sister should be "distinguished by Christlike charity,

a limpid simplicity of soul, heroic generosity, un-
swerving loyalty, prudent zeal, an orderly mind, gracious courtesy, an adaptable disposition, solid piety,
and the saving grace of a sense of humor." That is the
way Mother Mary Joseph, Foundress of the Mary-
knoll Sisters, would have a missionary Sister be. And
why not every Sister, whether at home or abroad?
Bishop Wade, American bishop of the Solomons,
listed three qualities he would like to have in the Sisters destined for his vicariate, the three "H's"—humor,
health, and holiness. And he seemed to think that if
holiness were lacking, but humor and health were
there, a few years of generous acceptance of another
"H" would make it sprout, namely, the humidity of
the Solomons. And that applies to many other places
in the world. It is said that the ability to laugh, especially at oneself, is practical humility or holiness in
action. The ideal Sister, at home and abroad, will
make it her endeavor to draw a picture of *sanctity
with a smile* in a life dynamized by the motivating
power of charity, love of God, and love of neighbor
for God's sake.

But you'll find the picture of *your* ideal Sister in
your rules!

*I often commit faults, and then I am so cast down
and discouraged that I almost give up everything.
Could you give me some solid advice?*

It seems that you need this bit of solid instruction
from *The Spiritual Combat,* by Scupoli:

"The tempter of pious souls often magnifies their
imperfections, persuading the faithful that they are
unfaithful to their duties, imperfect in confessions,
tepid at communion, and deficient in prayer. Thus
with various scruples he keeps them in constant alarm,

seeking to distract them from their exercises, as if God had forgotten or forsaken them. Nothing can be more false than to believe this, for the advantages arising from distractions, spiritual dryness, and the like, are innumerable, provided the soul comprehends and complies with what God expects of her in those circumstances. And God expects only patience and perseverance. For the prayers and exercises of a soul, deprived of all satisfaction in what she does, is the delight of the Almighty, according to St. Gregory.

"Particularly is such a soul pleasing to God if, notwithstanding its insensibility and apathy, it persists with courage. For the patience of such a soul is a prayer in itself, prevailing more with God than any prayers said with great emotional fervor. . . . Never forsake, therefore, any work of piety, however disinclined religiously you may be, unless you would comply with the wishes of Satan. . . . Spiritual barrenness and aridity bestow innumerable benefits upon the soul if accepted in the proper spirit of humility and prayer. . . . How utterly mistaken we are in thinking ourselves forsaken and abhorred by God Almighty, and deprived of the treasured tokens of His divine love; how erroneous to fancy ourselves punished by His anger, when actually we are favored by His goodness. Can we not see that the uneasiness that arises from such interior aridity can only spring from a desire of being altogether acceptable to God and zealous and fervent in His service? . . . We may well believe that these trials constitute a precious food by which God nourishes those whom He loves. Even though the temptation is so violent as to strike terror into our hearts, we shall derive innumerable blessings from it; for the blessings derived will be in proportion to the severity of our trial."

You must be on your guard against morbid introspection. This does not result from too much self-
knowledge. It is a sort of self-sided distortion of truth.
We never forget self, but we can so easily forget God.
Morbid introspection (a) forgets God, (b) centers attention on failure, (c) degrades contrition to self-centered disappointment, (d) scrupulously exaggerates
evil.

When you say that you have, for instance, a million
distractions in prayer, reflect that instead of a million
there is usually only one: yourself and your interests,
past, present, and to come.

*When things do not go my way, I am unhappy.
What should I do?*

It is well to keep in mind that there are certain
perennial mistakes which are made by most people,
not excluding religious. Two of these were already
noted by Cicero in the first century before Christ.
Reflect upon them. They are (1) the tendency to worry
about things which cannot be changed, and (2) at-
tempting to compel persons to believe and live as we
do. Then say the well-known prayer: "God give me
the courage to change what can be changed, the
serenity to bear what cannot be changed, and the wisdom to distinguish between the two."

Father Green, O.S.B., in *A Retreat for Religious,*
says apropos of this: "When things do not go according to our notions, we are tempted to become impatient. Why? Because we are too much attached to
our own opinion. This hardheaded clinging to our
own opinion is the root of the evil. We think that our
way is the only right way; but here is just where we
err. God's way is the only right way; and God's way is
the one pointed out by superiors, or by the majority,

or even by accidental circumstances. We must learn to see the finger of God in everything. We must learn, sooner or later, that the world is not governed by us or according to our notions. The sooner we get this fundamental truth into our heads, the better it will be for us, and the greater peace we will enjoy even in adversities."

My work does not seem to bring any results. My plans are consistently upset, and my hopes seem so futile; but in spite of it all I am quite happy and content. Don't you think I have quite a bit of virtue?

Well, yes, quite a bit, perhaps. But if instead of saying *in spite of it all* you had said *therefore*, then you would have delighted us. Then you would be like the Sister who said: "Father, God has *blessed* us again with a very severe trial." *Therefore*. It would be well for you to meditate on the beatitudes, the Savior's divine paradox. We here give them from the New Testament rendered from the original Greek by Father Kleist, S.J., and Father Lilly, C.M.:

> Blessed are the humble souls,
> for theirs is the kingdom of heaven.
> Blessed are the meek and gentle,
> for they will inherit the land.
> Blessed are the sorrowing,
> for they will be consoled.
> Blessed are those who hunger and thirst after holiness,
> for they will be fully satisfied.
> Blessed are the merciful,
> for they will have mercy shown to them.
> Blessed are the singlehearted,
> for they will see God.
> Blessed are the promoters of peace,

for they will rank as children of God.
Blessed are the victims of persecution for conscience'
sake,
for theirs is the kingdom of heaven.
Blessed are you when you are reviled, or persecuted,
or made a target for nothing but malicious lies—for
my sake.
Rejoice; yes, leap for joy; a rich reward awaits you
in heaven.
(Matt. 5:3-12.)

The expression *humble souls,* says a footnote, generally rendered "in spirit," means that persons of low
rank in life, downtrodden, oppressed, mean in the
eyes of the world, are blessed if they accept their lot
willingly and with due submission to Divine Providence.

*I'm going to be so very good now that I'll be en-
tirely free from the passions of anger, lust, fear, and all
the rest. Don't you think that's a commendable and
heroic resolution?*

If you maintain that that can be done, you are holding to an error condemned by the Church. Rather
keep waging a truceless war and preserve yourself in
peaceful abandonment to God. "God permits the re-
bellions of the sensitive appetite, both in the matter of
anger and lust, to continue in us. . . . The passions
only die with ourselves. . . . However, we should not
be troubled at feeling their presence, because our perfection consists in combatting them, and we cannot
combat them unless we feel them. Our victory depends not on being insensible to their suggestions, but
on refusing to consent to them. . . . Divine love is
saddened by nothing except sin; it is rather our own
self-love which would have us exempt from the labor

involved in resistance to our passions. It is really the trouble of making the necessary effort that disquiets us," says St. Francis de Sales. That is, unless it be the humiliation and shame caused by our experiencing certain evil motions.

Our very faults are no obstacle to our progress if we rise from them promptly and contritely, and without scruple and disquietude proceed on our way, trying to do better. They impart to us, according to St. Gregory, "the very uncommon perfection which consists in knowing that we are not perfect." Without God we can do nothing. Consider the child just born and the dying man. These two extremes of life mark its true character. Practice this poverty of spirit.

I wish to have a cross, since we must take up the cross daily and follow the Savior; but I prefer one of my own choice. Is that all right?

You may complain of your afflictions to God, but lovingly and with moderation. Our Lord is pleased when we talk to Him about the tribulations He sends us, as little children to their dear mother when she has chastised them. But when it is necessary to drink the chalice of bitterness, give your free consent by saying from the heart to God: "Not my will, but Thine be done."

St. Francis de Sales further says to St. Jane de Chantal: "You wish to have a cross, but you would prefer one of your own choice. That is not the right disposition. The cross I desire both for myself and for you is none other than the cross of Jesus Christ. Let Him send us all the aridities He pleases, provided He preserves us in His holy love. We can never serve Him well unless we serve him in the manner He requires to be served. Now, He requires that you serve Him

without relish, without feeling, with repugnances and
distress of mind. Such service does not give you much
satisfaction, but it greatly pleases Him; it is not to
your taste, but it is in accordance with His good-
pleasure. Imagine that you were never to be delivered
from your affliction. You would then say to God:
'Lord, I am Thine! If my sufferings give Thee satisfaction, increase both their number and their duration!' . . . Make friends with your troubles as if you
were destined to live always together. And you will
find that when you have ceased to think of your deliv-
erance, God will think of it."

*Do you not think that religious ought to adapt
themselves more to modern conditions and not stick
so much to tradition and to customs and things that
were "always the practice" in their respective congregations or orders?*

In the year 1950 was held in Rome under the
auspices of the Sacred Congregation of Religious, with
the approbation of Pope Pius XII, a General Congress
on the States of Perfection.

The theme of this Congress (the *Acta et Documenta*
of which have since been published) may be succintly
stated thus: the renewal of the primitive spirit of
religious institutes adapted to the needs of the present
day.

But it was repeatedly stressed that the adaptation to
modern needs is not a mitigation of the primitive
spirit and regular observance. Religious are both to
renew their interior spirit and to adapt themselves to
the urgent needs of the present day. It is a bold challenge: *both* a renewal of the spirit of the founders *and*
a certain adjustment in view of the conditions of modern life are necessary. But none of the essential ele-

ments of religious life and spirit may be changed. "Renew your spirit or die!"

Every institute should be a living continuation of the mind and spirit of the founder. Religious are to return to the primitive spirit of the founder, to an exact observance of the constitutions, and to a promotion of common life and fraternal charity. In every instance the superior (for theirs is also this weighty responsibility) should act in the same way as the founder would act were he alive today.

Sometimes I have such a distaste for prayer and spiritual things. What should I then do?

Dryness, distaste, lack of consolation in prayer— these things are very valuable, a hidden favor from heaven, and should make the performance of your spiritual exercises even more dear to you, as being more meritorious. As Father Green, O.S.B., succinctly reminds us: "One meditation made with a painful effort and a ceaseless fight against rebellious nature, is of greater value and wins richer reward than a week's meditations made amid the sweets of heavenly consolation. There is more real love of God and self-denial in it."

There is sometimes also darkness in the spiritual life, accompanied by the most awful and violent temptations. There may be foul representations against purity, even in regard to holy persons, saints, and the Savior Himself. There may be temptations against faith. Or most horrible blasphemies may rush to the mind and at times formulate themselves with such articulate clearness that the soul is at a loss to judge whether it uttered them or not. But in the midst of such temptations the soul is praying; and it clings to God with the superior part of the will. With the

Savior it cries out: "My God, my God, why hast Thou forsaken me?" knowing all the while that it has not been really forsaken.

Then there are delusions and scrupulosity. Confide in your confessor as regards these and obey him as you would the Savior Himself.

I certainly do not want to be a lukewarm religious; but isn't there such a thing as the golden mean? Why insist upon being a perfectly good religious?

Let's not fool ourselves, as so many religious are wont to do. Generally speaking, our lives are satiny and velvety compared with the lives of the saints, indeed even when compared with the lives of many people living in the world, who very often have a hard time of it.

Mediocrity will not do. You would not want to say you are lukewarm; but are you listless, without much fervor, easy-going, mediocre? That sounds like lukewarmness. Mediocre means ordinary, middling, indifferent, commonplace, second-rate, undistinguished. Nothing flattering about any of those words. Mediocre religious! If you try to rest satisfied with the golden mean, as you call it, you will not only not make progress—you will go backward.

Most of us would do well to examine ourselves as regards these three miseries: (1) idle thoughts—what thoughts the mind does grind through in a single day, what a heap of chaff; and it is a law of nature that we think of what we love; (2) useless desires—don't hurry over what you are about in order to get to something else, but attend to present duties instead of future fancies; (3) needless anxieties—but one thing is necessary, namely, to love God with one's whole heart. Says St. Teresa: "Let nothing disturb thee, let nothing affright thee. All things are passing, God only is lasting."

What is the meaning of holy abandonment? Is it a very great virtue?

Abandonment is an act of trustful love by which we throw ourselves into the arms of Providence as a child throws itself into the arms of its mother. Think of a child when it feels it is in danger running to its mother and snuggling contentedly in her arms. Abandonment simply means to deprive oneself of one's own will in order to give it up to God. It means to have such faith in the goodness and love of God that we receive with equal readiness from His hands joys and sorrows, prosperity and adversity. It means to believe that God is managing our affairs with admirable wisdom and love even "when He seems to be destroying us and annihilating us, when He frustrates our holiest designs, when He exposes us to calumny, obscures all our lights in prayer, dries up our devotion and fervor with aridities, ruins our health with infirmities and languors, reduces us to incapacity for doing anything at all."

St. Alphonsus says: "Abandonment is itself an act of the most perfect love of God that can be produced; it is of more value than a thousand fasts and disciplines. For he who gives his substance in alms, his blood in disciplines, his sustenance in fasting, gives but a portion of what he possesses; whereas he who gives his will to God gives himself, gives all, so that he can say with truth: 'Lord, I am poor, but I give Thee as much as I can; having resigned to Thee my will, I have nothing more to offer Thee.' "

Yes, it is a very great virtue. By it we identify our wills with the will of God, so that of two wills we make but one, in the sense that we never will anything but what He wills, our wills being lost in His. This, as St. Alphonsus says, is the summit of all perfection.

Speaking of the will of God, we might recall that it is the regulative, or the signified will, e.g., commandments, precepts, counsels; for religious in particular, the vows, rules, and prescriptions of superiors. All those are for them the signified will of God, the will of God made known, *as made known.*

Then there is the will of the divine good-pleasure, or the operative will of God, i.e., the universal principle of being, of life, and of action. Everything happens because of its behests; nothing happens independently of its decrees: all effects from the First Cause, all motions from the Prime Mover.

As a child walks when its mother puts it on the ground and allows itself to be taken up again into her arms when she wishes, "in just the same way the soul that loves the divine good-pleasure permits herself to be carried and yet walks, too, by fulfilling with great solicitude all that appertains to God's signified will," says St. Francis de Sales.

Recall the celebrated maxim of the same St. Francis: "Desire nothing, ask nothing, refuse nothing." (But this, he explicitly says, is not applicable to the practice of virtue.) It can be applied to offices and employments in the community, to sicknesses, consolations, afflictions. But we have the right to form desires and make petitions with regard to everything that comes from the good-pleasure of God, so long as His will does not manifest itself as absolute and irrevocable. However, we are not bound, *ordinarily,* to use that right.

In this connection it is well to remember also, as Pope Leo XIII says: "There is not and cannot be a truly passive virtue." We have power of free choice, and God will not sanctify us without our cooperation.

Practice conformity to the will of God even in the smallest things: the humiliation resulting from forgetfulness; that coming from awkwardness; the annoyance caused by a fly, a barking dog, the noise of heavy traffic outside the window, the roar of planes overhead; hurting oneself by bumping against something or cutting oneself accidentally; no light; no heat; getting stuck in prayer. And what opportunities for practicing this conformity you will find in the differences of character, the contradictions, and the thousand and one other things that are inseparable from community life.

Perhaps it is asking too much, but I would like some very simple means of loving God very much, and my neighbor too, for God's sake.

Loving God means to do what He wants us to do and graciously to accept whatever He permits to happen to us. Loving the neighbor means to wish him well because he is Christ's representative, according to the Savior's own words: "Whatsoever you do to one of these, My least brethren, you do unto Me."

A loving soul will often think: "How can I please God in all that I do?" Thus you will always do well what you do, mindful of His presence, seeking His silent approbation.

Loving God means to imitate the Savior, who went about doing good. Be kind and charitable always, at work, during recreations, in conversations, in company. Always make everything as easy as you can for those who are around you, provided you can do so without neglecting your duties. Suppress every gesture, even every expression which might betray im-

patience or displeasure, crushing such feelings immediately and making it your aim never to show yourself
sensitive, sulky, offended—all in imitation of the
Savior. When you are tempted to think or speak or
act unkindly toward others, keep repeating from the
heart, as long as the temptation lasts, this little prayer:
"Lord, make them happy, here and hereafter." That
is what you want for yourself, happiness here and
hereafter; and thus you will be loving your neighbor
as yourself for God's sake.

Make it your particular examen to show special
kindness in thought, word, and deed toward those
with whom you live, especially toward those who do
not seem to like you very well or for whom you have
feelings of aversion.

Often thank God for His many graces to you; and
do not forget that one fervent *Deo gratias* when He
sends you things that you do not like is more meritorious than many when all goes well. We must have our
daily crosses. The Master said: "If any man will come
after Me, let him take up his cross daily and follow
Me." This little prayer of Cardinal Merry del Val,
now indulgenced (300 days each time), will appeal to
you greatly: "My dearest Jesus, teach me to be patient,
when all the day long my heart is troubled by little,
but vexatious, crosses."

You want simple means of loving God very much.
Why, there are so many at hand for you. Keep your
vows, be an observant religious by keeping all the
rules. Then, out of gratitude to God, who has been so
infinitely good to you, ceaselessly aspire to perform
your spiritual exercises well, especially your daily
meditation, Holy Mass, Holy Communion, the
Rosary, your Office.

Again, in your daily life always try to be as recollected as possible; make many mental ejaculations every day, or whisper them with the lips, if you prefer; always try to attain holy indifference (as long as it's for God's glory); never cease to deplore your sins; carefully guard against laxity even in small matters; adhere faithfully to your particular examen; never grow tired of gently and sensibly banishing distractions in prayer; always make your monthly preparation for death especially well; make the way of the cross every day if time permits; renew your holy vows privately each day; make frequent spiritual communions and often unite yourself with the Savior offering Himself in Holy Mass throughout the world. Make each day count for heaven.

Is it true that there are special dangers to religious observance in our time and country?

In this regard there are especially three dangers which threaten religious life in the United States and tend to the loss of the primitive spirit:

1. Naturalism. Only a serious attempt to live the regular life, to excel in religious observance according to the spirit of the institute as ordained by its founder, only a deepening of the interior life and a supernatural motivation will preserve the religious from naturalism.

2. A lack or the loss of the spirit of mortification. Here again there must be a more scrupulous observance of the constitutions and a revival of the primitive spirit of the religious institute. There are three kinds of mortification, to give one division: (a) Involuntary, absolute abandonment to the will of God in whatever He sends us. This kind we cannot avoid. These are things we cannot dodge. This is the highest kind of mortification when humbly and lovingly submitted

to. (b) Voluntary, second degree: this, let us say, for religious means the observance of the rules. Dodge these and you commit the fault of not making use of a great means of striving after that perfection which you have promised to strive after. (c) Additional voluntary mortifications. These are not of obligation and may be omitted without fault.

3. Excessive activity. Here apply also the words addressed by Pope Pius XII to the clergy of the world in his apostolic exhortation *Menti Nostrae:* "We cannot abstain from expressing our pre-occupation and our anxiety for those who on account of the special circumstance of the moment have become so engulfed in the vortex of external activity that they neglect the chief duty of the priest, his own sanctification. . . . The heresy of action is that activity which is not based upon the help of grace and does not make a constant use of the means necessary to the pursuit of sanctity given us by Christ. In the same way, nevertheless, We have deemed it timely to stimulate to the activities of the ministry those who, shut up in themselves and almost diffident of the efficacy of divine aid, do not labor to the best of their ability to make the spirit of Christianity penetrate daily life in all those ways demanded by our times."

Here again is the bold challenge: renew your interior spirit, the primitive spirit of the institute, and adapt yourselves at the same time to the urgent needs of the present day.

Since we have spoken so much about religious observance in this reply, it is quite in place here to quote the striking words of St. Bonaventure in reference to the keeping of the rules. If all religious would live according to this dictum of a great saint and religious, the desires of the Holy See as regards the preservation of the primitive spirit of the institute would be fully realized:

"I have not entered religion to live as others live, but to live as they ought to live, according to the spirit of the institute and in perfect observance of the rules. That is why, on entering religion, I was given the rules to read and not the lives of others. I took them for the direction of the life I should lead. I ought to observe them all, even if I saw no one else observe them."

Like St. John Berchmans, you should be able to take your crucifix, your rosary, and your book of rules in your hands and say: "In life these three were the dearest to me; with these I will gladly die."

Why do we find religious who, after years of observance of their rules, still fail upon the least trial or contradiction that thwarts their favorite inclination?

The reason for this, no doubt, is that such religious forget that the foundation of sanctity lies in subduing the passions and in dying to self. There is so much inordinate self-love in the best of us. Many, indeed, pray much, multiply their religious practices, even practice corporal penances; but they lose at least a portion of the fruits thereof by not striving to die to self. The least little thing upsets them beyond all measure. As long as self-love remains uncontrolled in their souls, as long as sensitiveness, selfishness, and sensuality are not duly repressed, such remain blind and deceived and, their good works being marred, their devotions are liable to delusions. They crawl along in the dust of their imperfections.

What should such religious do? Let them renounce their own lights, their own will, their self-love. Then they will arrive at the liberty of the children of God.

In this connection we might ask: "Where are the religious who desire to have superiors who exercise them by trials and who apply strong remedies, as so many of the monks of old desired?"

I would appreciate your advising me if there is a book in existence on fraternal charity and fraternal correction and allied topics. If one is not sure of one's prudence and tact, is it not better to practice fraternal correction by means of prayer and, as far as possible, by good example?

In *The Practice of Christian Perfection* by Alphonsus Rodriguez, S.J., there is an excellent treatise on fraternal charity in the first volume; and the last treatise in the third volume is on fraternal correction. Yes. If you are not sure of your prudence and tact, substitute prayer and good example for fraternal correction strictly so called. Example speaks louder than words.

In his introduction to *The Saving Sense,* Father W. Coleman Nevils, S.J., writes of the work mentioned: "Among the books prescribed as spiritual reading for Jesuit novices is *Christian Perfection* by Alphonsus Rodriguez; at least a half-hour each day for two years is spent in the perusal of this marvelous book; by many it is regarded as the most extraordinary of its class. It is quaint in matter and style; it has been translated into practically all languages and is still held in highest esteem, not only in the Society of Jesus, but by all Religious Orders and Congregations. It has never had a rival." Father Faber calls the work "an inestimable treasure of the Church." St. Frances Cabrini drew up a list of five books as constituting a sufficient spiritual library for her congregation; one of the five was Rodriguez.

The book has gone through more than fifty editions in Spanish and has been translated into at least twenty languages, including Arabian, Tamil, and Chinese. The most recent English translator was Father Joseph Rickaby, S.J., who translated it straight from the Spanish. The authorized American edition of that translation, in three large volumes, with large restful print, was put out by Loyola University Press, Chicago, Illinois.

The Practice of Perfection and Christian Virtues (the complete title) is primarily and almost exclusively an ascetical, not a mystical work. But it is not "anti-mystical."

As Father Augustine Klaas, S.J., says in *Review for Religious* for May, 1944, where he has a magnificent article on this book and its author: "A few points of his doctrine can be legitimately contested and even impugned. Some of his examples and anecdotes are considered today to be lacking in good taste: many of these have been excised in recent editions. But, after all, these are only minor flaws in an author whose work is a masterpiece of spiritual writing that has successfully stood the test of time, and that even with readers who are more than ordinarily critical and exacting. It is today the most widely used spiritual textbook of religious the world over. A definitive critical edition would indeed be very welcome."

With *Meditations on the Mysteries of Our Holy Faith* by Louis de Ponte, S.J., from the original Spanish (in five volumes, now out of print) for meditation and *The Practice of Perfection and Christian Virtues* by Alphonsus Rodriguez for spiritual reading, plus, of course, the Bible, the Missal, and *The Imitation of Christ,* and the book of rules, any religious will have a sufficient library for constant growth in sanctity unto life eternal.

What is abandonment as recommended in the spiritual life?

Abandonment (loving indifference as long as it's for God's glory) is a filial disposition to accept whatever God may will, with the sweet tranquillity of a babe in its mother's arms. A babe leaves to its mother the care of moving, acting, and willing in its behalf. Here we might think of the Baby Jesus in Mary's arms.

We might further illustrate by saying that abandonment is:

1. A clean sheet of paper on which God may write what He pleases.

2. A liquid, which has no shape of its own, but assumes the shape of the vessel in which it is put.

3. A ball of wax in the hands of God, which He can shape as He pleases.

4. A beast of burden (e.g., a pack horse) that is loaded by its master as the master wishes, having nothing to decide about the quality or quantity of its burden, and that goes or stops at the will of the master.

5. A loving *Yes* to God's holy will. "Yes, dear God, I will do it at once." "Yes, dear God, I accept this gladly."

6. An ardent *Amen* to everything that God wills in our regard.

7. A servant continually and happily attending upon the Sovereign Master and heedful of His every wish.

8. A voyager embarked upon the ship of Divine Providence and sailing for the eternal shore.

But remember that in all this neither prudence,

prayer, desire, personal effort, nor sensibility to pain are excluded.

Nothing happens without the will of God. If my neighbor injures me, am I to see the will of God in that?

It is a never-ending source of edification and wonder to read the story of Joseph in the Book of Genesis. Near the end of that story we hear Joseph saying to his brothers: "And God sent me before you, that you may be preserved upon the earth and may have food to live. Not by your counsel was I sent hither, but by the will of God" (Gen. 45:7, 8).

Yes. If my neighbor injures me, I am to see the will of God in it; for in such things God wills to punish the guilty and try the just. But if the person who injures me sins by inflicting that injury, it is God's permissive will that I am to see. In sin there are two elements, the material element and the formal element. Since nothing can move or act without God, He is certainly the cause of the material or physical act of sin, by His concurrence, and in this sense He permits it. The formal element of sin consists in not conforming to what one knows to be the will of God. This lack of conformity in my act to the will of God known to me is really not an act at all. It is the negation of an act, a defect, the lack of something (like the hole in a doughnut), which needs no help from God, is not caused by God, but is merely permitted, tolerated. God concurs in the material act of sin only; He does not concur in the sin as such, but only permits it in so far as it cannot be prevented without violence to free will. Why does He permit it, tolerate it? Because this is demanded by the nobility of man, who has a free will. This permission, of course, is not an authorization of sin; for God detests sin and only postpones its punishment. In the meantime it enters into His designs to draw good out of evil in favor of the elect. In this connection, consider the Passion of Christ. For this end He makes use of the weakness and malice of men, even their worst transgressions.

When someone injures me in any way, or even annoys me, it is the will of God that I bear it. Though it is something negative on the part of my neighbor, it is a cause of merit for me.

Sometimes I am in trouble and don't know what to do; and even if I kneel before Jesus in the Eucharist and tell Him, or in Holy Communion, I don't arrive at any decision. What should I do?

Of course, we do and we should kneel before Jesus in the Blessed Sacrament and ask Him to tell us what to do in the problems that perplex us, just as when we stand in need of special enlightenment we naturally pray to the Holy Spirit: "God the Holy Ghost, have mercy on us." *"Veni, Sancte Spiritus! Veni, Creator Spiritus!"*

But we should also keep in mind that Jesus is not in the Blessed Sacrament chiefly for the purpose of solving doubts and enlightening consciences, but to be the divine life and nourishment of our souls.

So He has given us someone who can speak in His stead. That someone may be the spiritual director, or it may be the confessor, or it may be the superior. We should consult those whom God has placed over us. In them we shall find Him, especially in those who have been officially appointed over us. His presence is also in the power that governs us. "He who hears you, hears Me."

*What is one to think of a Sister who is always ex-
tremely severe and solemn and unsmiling in outward
mien, taciturn and unapproachable and seemingly
wrapped in sorrowful recollection? Is this a special
kind of holiness?*

It might be. It is possible that she is crushed in
spirit by the sinfulness of the world and the lack of
religious observance in the convent. Sometimes we
read that, though the Divine Savior wept, it is no-
where recorded in Holy Writ that He smiled or
laughed. There is only one picture of Jesus which
shows Him with a smile on His face, as far as we can
remember. But we think He must have smiled often,
especially on the little children—and on those big and
sometimes "dumb" children who were His chosen
apostles.

Sometimes, however, long-faced piety is only bil-
iousness; and many a sad-eyed visionary needs only a
liver regulator. Spiritual desolation, dissatisfaction
with self, and aridity may be, perhaps, only dyspepsia,
or sour stomach.

A religious such as you mention is often rather
nervous, touchy, excitable also. At any rate, we would
advise her, and all Sisters, to take more exercise, to
remember the *ora et labora,* and to get plenty of
activity and fresh air. This will be good for both the
physical and the spiritual life. Often enough it is a
real act of self-denial to get out of a cozy room into
the fresh air and to make the body that is getting too
much inactivity take sufficient exercise. Go out, even
if it would be nice to stay in!

Nervousness is often due to overfeeding and under-
exercising. Suspicion and envy and jealousy often dis-

appear before fresh air. And scruples are often only a manifestation of a nervous disposition.

Sometimes I think that I am unfaithful to good inspirations. There is so much good that I could do which I don't do. What is to be said about this?

You mean that you could do so many little things that you do not do. You could, for instance, kneel more and sit less in the chapel, could kneel without support, could fold your hands devoutly instead of holding them comfortably, could say more ejaculatory prayers, gain more indulgences, deny yourself more at table by not taking something you would like or taking a dish you do not like so much, could be more friendly, and so forth.

To this often unspoken query of many a good soul, Bishop Hedley in a retreat for priests replied: "But I would like to say that we are not obliged to do the most mortifying thing in small matters. This is not unfaithfulness to grace, but *good*—on the reflex principle that it is better not to be too anxious in things that are not of precept. But this does not apply to rule or to obedience, or to anything that is clearly a duty— like the avoiding of venial sin, even at the cost of suffering and self-imposed penance."

What are some of the things you would suggest that I do in order to spend at least one day as perfectly as possible?

Live in the present; do not worry about the past and the future, but love God *now*.

Make your half hour or hour of meditation a happy time of rest and relaxation in the Lord. Make up your mind that this is going to be a happy hour, one in which your every breath seems to be the prayer: "O most holy Trinity, living by Thy grace in my soul, sanctify me more and more. Abide with me, Lord; be my true joy."

In this same spirit of quiet and selflessness assist at Mass and receive Holy Communion. "Lord, for to-morrow and its wants I do not pray: give me Thy love and Thy grace just for today."

Meditate quietly on the respective mysteries while you say your daily rosary.

Let your spiritual reading be done slowly, thought-fully, meditatively, putting into it effort, thought, and concentration.

See to it that all the little prayers, in addition to your office, if you recite that, are said with real atten-tion and devotion. Because they are short, they should be more intense. This applies to morning and evening prayers, prayers before and after meals, the examina-tion of conscience, every sign of the cross and every genuflection that you make, every aspiration and ejaculation. This applies above all to your little visits to the Blessed Sacrament and to your brief way of the cross.

Carefully follow the order of the day, adjusting yourself to things as they are and not for a moment expecting them to fit in with your own desires, except to the extent that you want what God wants.

See Jesus in others and think, speak, and act in their regard as you would toward Him; and be so charitable and good that others may look up and see not only you, but Jesus also. In addition, do some-body a good turn and see to it that you are not found out. In honor of the five wounds do five things that you don't want to do.

Do not criticize one bit; say only what is good about others, mindful of the words of Holy Writ: "If any

man offend not in speech, the same is a perfect man."
In addition, speak low and courteously, observing religious silence according to the rules in every way.

If your feelings are hurt, do not show it. If you hurt the feelings of another in any way, be sure to say "I'm sorry" before the day is done.

Do not try to make anybody better, or improve upon anybody, or regulate the conduct of anybody, except yourself. You are the one who is trying today to live as perfectly as possible—*quam perfectissime*.

Then, at the end of your perfect day, as you glance over your observance of your vows, renew with all your heart those solemn promises of poverty, chastity, and obedience according to the Constitutions.

How can I cultivate the spirit and habit of practically continuous prayer?

Always begin your prayers with a sign of the cross that is truly devout, not slipshod, slovenly, mechanical, something little better than a caricature. And think each time of what it means. Make every genuflection properly and devoutly, accompanied by aspirations of various kinds, like acts of adoration, thanksgiving for Holy Communion, spiritual communion; for here too you must beware of the slipshod, the slovenly, the careless, the thoughtless. Bow to the crucifix as you enter or leave the room, looking with sympathy on the tortured body of your Savior. In a word, attend carefully to all the many little religious practices which are usually performed so thoughtlessly, even irreverently, lest you lose religious ground and become ever more religiously insensitive. Constant concentration and drilling in all these things, instead of trifling and drifting, will fill your religious life with spiritual definiteness and exactness. Just

make much of the little religious exercises and practices, appreciate them, cultivate them with unbroken
continuity; make yourself do it day after day, and you
will succeed gloriously and become a master in the
spirit and art of prayer. On the contrary, if you drift,
and trifle, and fluctuate, and do not concentrate on
definite practices, you will not get anywhere in your
prayer life.

To all this add the practice of making devout
aspirations and ejaculations in all your prayers and in
all your work. Make scores of those devoutly each
day, and you will soon be continually walking in the
presence of God.

*There once was a religious who made just one big
resolution during the annual retreat, which she wrote
down in capitals. It read: mind your own business.
Was that a good resolution? Is it well to make only
one?*

Ordinarily we make many resolutions during the
retreat. They come to us spontaneously while listening to the considerations or during our meditative
spiritual reading. They are made in passing, so to
speak—and often broken or forgotten in the same way.
But it is good to make them; for in meditation we
should always strive to arrive at affections and resolutions. It is a good thing for many to write down the
thoughts that struck them during the consideration,
the lights, the resolves. But this should generally be
done, not while the retreat master is speaking, but
afterwards, whenever one has the leisure. To do this
after each conference or meditation means to have a
brief personal resume of the retreat for reconsidera-
tion on the monthly recollection day or at other times.

However, in addition to that, each one should make

one or two or three big resolutions, preferably one.
And that should be a frontal attack upon some sin or
imperfection that is harming one's spiritual life. It
may have to do with charity, with the observance of
one of the vows, with the performance of the daily
spiritual exercises, or with something else that is holding one back on the way to God.

About the resolution you mention, Father Gabriel,
S.J., says: "How much good we could accomplish and
how much merit we could gain, if we would never
meddle with anything or anybody, least of all with
government or superiors, but would strictly *mind our
own business* and give our undivided attention and
energy to the performance of our duties, to the up-
rooting of our vices, without presuming to criticize
or striving to correct what has not been committed to
our charge."

Another big resolution could well be this: I will
seek in all things to please God. Or this: I will think
more of God and not so much of my petty self. Or
this: I will make up with so and so, speak to her, be
friendly toward her always. Or this: I will see Jesus
in others and think and speak and act accordingly.
Or what have you? The big resolution of the retreat
is so personal that it is like a matter of conscience for
each one. There may be as many different such resolves as there are retreatants.

*What instructions would you suggest to encourage
religious to be well-mannered, courteous, polite?*

Instructions in politeness are not to be neglected in
the training of religious. There are various excellent
manuals on this subject. It is an important one because, as *The Imitation of Christ* says: "How pleasant

and sweet it is to see brethren fervent and devout, well-mannered and well-disciplined!"

What we ordinarily call politeness is really a blend, a divine mixture, a delicious balm, of humility, mortification, and Christian charity.

Religious well know the dictum of St. Paul: "Whether you eat, or whether you drink, or whatever you do, do all for the glory of God. Religious, whose whole appearance presumably breathes modesty and sweet simplicity, because they are the favored followers of Him who was meek and humble of heart, often meditate on these other words of the Apostle of the Gentiles: "One of the principal fruits of the Spirit is modesty, which ought to shine in all your conduct; clothe yourselves, then, with exemplary modesty, as suits the elect and well beloved of Jesus."

Religious may appeal to the saints in their defense, should it happen that they may be reproached for being too polite:

St. Augustine says: "Let there be nothing in our exterior not in harmony with the sanctity of our vocation and the edification we owe one another: our gait, the perfect adjustment of our garb, the various movements of our person—let there be nothing in us that would wound the eyes of any one, but let all breathe holiness."

St. Gregory of Nazianzen says: "Wherever the divine Master is found, there also ought to be and, in fact, is found admirable modesty."

St. Ambrose: "Let your exterior be perfectly composed and well regulated, without affectation or the least artifice; for nothing affected delights God."

St. Isidore of Pelusium: "Let all our steps be marked with the coin of good-breeding, and let there be in us nothing eager, nothing petulant, nothing brusque, nothing that savors of ignorance."

St. Bernard: "I conjure you, if you love Mary and if you wish to please her, endeavor to imitate her remarkable exterior modesty. Preserve always a joyous, serene, open, tranquil countenance without embarrassment or constraint."

Indeed, at anyone who would insinuate that they are not to be well-mannered and well-disciplined, religious could hurl these words of St. Bonaventure: "It is only the extravagant, the fools who dare maintain that no condescension, no courtesy is due to the neighbor; that the merit and qualities of others deserve no consideration; and that incivility and rudeness may pass for virtue in religion."

Incivility and rudeness—what examples of that could be adduced? Perhaps sneezing and coughing without the discreet use of a handkerchief, unsuppressed coughing and blowing of the nose, spitting and yawning and sighing aloud, lack of attention to the wants of others at table, and such like incongruities.

To be considerate of the feelings of others always is charity.

As a religious I have the obligation to strive after perfection. I would like to become perfect. What should I do?

How surely and how easily we religious can become perfect by keeping the rules conscientiously. All of them always, came home to us with great force some time ago when we read the following words of Cardinal Newman:

"If you ask me what you are to do in order to become perfect, I say: 1) Do not lie in bed beyond the

due time of rising. 2) Give your first thoughts to God.
3) Make a really good visit to the Blessed Sacrament.
4) Say the Angelus devoutly. 5) Eat and drink to God's
glory. 6) Say the Rosary well. 7) Be always recollected.
8) Keep out bad thoughts. 9) Make your evening
meditation well. 10) Examine your conscience daily."

We wonder how many religious there are who will
read these lines thoughtfully, examine themselves
thereon carefully, and then not exclaim within themselves: "Why, how simple! All these things I have
been doing for a long time now, and many, many
other things besides!"

Really now? How about your promptness in rising?
and giving your first thoughts to God? and being
fervent in your visits? and saying the Angelus devoutly? and eating and drinking to God's glory? and
saying the Rosary well? and being always recollected?
and keeping out bad thoughts? and making your meditation (whenever you make it) well? and how about
that examination of conscience? when did you last
make it truly well?

And then the many other things besides: Silence?
charity? poverty? chastity? obedience?

How can I best live always in the presence of God?

You can do that best by remembering that if you
are in sanctifying grace (and every religious will make
sure always to be in sanctifying grace), the three
divine Persons, Father, Son, and Holy Spirit, dwell
within your soul. This is a mysterious but a real presence, of which Christ says: "If any man love me . . .
my Father will love him and we will come to him and
make our abode with him" (John 14:23). By grace
God dwells in the soul as a friend, a guest, and a
lover; already by grace is begun that intimate union

between God and the creature which will be con-
summated in the glory of heaven.

Of course, God is everywhere, as you know. He is
everywhere, as St. Thomas says, "by His presence,
inasmuch as all things are naked and open to His
eyes; by His essence, inasmuch as He is present to all
as the cause of their being." But He is present in the
just in a special manner; the divine Persons reside by
grace in the just soul as in a temple in a most intimate
way.

The fact of this indwelling is a dogma of the faith.
"Know you not that you are the temple of God, and
that the Spirit of God dwelleth in you?" (I Cor. 3:16)
It is not only the Holy Spirit, however, but all three
Persons who dwell within the soul in sanctifying
grace; but this inhabitation is appropriated in a spe-
cial way to Him because the Holy Spirit is the infinite
Love of the Supreme Good.

What a consoling thought this is. We have dwelling
within us the Holy Spirit, and the Blessed Trinity,
the source of all the virtues, gifts, and fruits bestowed
by the Holy Spirit upon men. And even our mortal
bodies, since they are the temples of the Blessed
Trinity, are in a special manner made holy, and
sacred, and worthy of the general resurrection.

What should follow from this fact that we are God's
living tabernacles, from the fact that His presence in
us is real? He is as really, truly, and substantially present in the soul that is in the state of grace as Christ is
really, truly, and substantially present in the tabernacle of the altar. When we enter the church, we are
always conscious (or ought to be) of the near presence
of Jesus in the tabernacle. So, too, we ought to be conscious always of the presence of the Holy Spirit within
us.

We look upon the precious fifteen minutes (Pujiula, 1948) or so of the real presence of Christ within ourselves after receiving Holy Communion, and rightly so, as the time in which we can constantly grow in sanctifying grace, and we lovingly entertain our Eucharistic Guest. But the Holy Spirit abides within us as in His temple as long as we are in the state of grace and, for the most part, we neglect Him.

We ought to visit the Blessed Trinity dwelling in our hearts, as we visit Jesus in the Blessed Sacrament. Both visits should be paid frequently during the day. However, a visit to the Blessed Sacrament is not always possible; but a visit to the Most Holy Trinity dwelling in us as in a temple is always and at all times possible, and it is sweet and consoling indeed.

That is the way in which you can best live in the presence of God. St. Elizabeth of the Trinity once cried out: "I have found heaven upon the earth since heaven is God and I have God in my soul!"

St. Teresa of Avila says: "If you try to remember that you possess a guest of such majesty within your soul you will not become engrossed, as you do, in the things of earth. If I had known before that a great King dwells in the little palace of my soul, I would not have left Him alone so often."

Three indulgenced prayers which will help you to remember often your divine Guest are the following:

O Holy Spirit, sweet Guest of my soul, abide with me and grant that I may always abide with Thee. (300 days)

God the Holy Ghost, have mercy on us. (500 days)

May the grace of the Holy Spirit enlighten our senses and our hearts. (500 days)

For each of the last two a plenary indulgence can be gained once a month under the usual conditions if

they are devoutly recited every day for a whole month.
(*Raccolta*, nos. 278, 279, 280)

Say the *Veni, Creator Spiritus* and the *Veni, Sancte Spiritus* every day. Yes; He dwells in the souls of the just; but, save for a limited number of souls, how spiritually void and empty the world is today. How many, too, have banished Him by mortal sin. But we call upon Him also to come to us with whom He already is as in His temple, inasmuch as we wish to be His, not only by the gift of sanctifying grace, but also by a constant increase in the three theological virtues of faith, hope, and charity; by a richer communication of His seven gifts: wisdom, understanding, counsel, fortitude, knowledge, piety, and fear of the Lord; by a more abundant harvest of the fruits of the Holy Ghost: charity, joy, peace, patience, benignity, goodness, long-suffering, mildness, faith, modesty, continency, and chastity; by enabling us to practice more perfectly the eight beatitudes and merit their rewards; and by helping us to excel in the moral virtues, chief of which are prudence, justice, fortitude, and temperance.

Yes, though the Holy Spirit dwells within us as a friend, enriching the soul with wonderful gifts and protecting it by His loving providence, we do not always devote ourselves with all our powers to God. Hence we cry, even while He is with us (for venial sins and imperfections do not drive Him away), *Veni*. Come and take away all worldliness, all self-deception, all sham, every taint of vanity and pride, ambition, envy, jealousy, uncharitableness, rivalry, hatred, stubbornness, self-will, habits of disobedience, disedifying negligence, irregularity.

The Holy Spirit is invisibly present in the soul which is in sanctifying grace, yet really, truly, and substantially. There is a striking passage in *The Interior Castle* in which St. Theresa expresses this realization of God in a very vivid manner: "It is as if, when we were with other people in a well-lighted room, some one were to darken it by closing the shutters; we should feel certain that the others were still there, though we were unable to see them."

You want to live in the presence of God. It is often lack of knowledge such as the above which keeps a soul back from a sense of God's presence which would fill it with joy and lead it on, with giant strides, toward true perfection of life. What a pity to be thus held back. Meditate on the above answer. Resolve. Then put your resolution into practice.

II

THE RELIGIOUS LIFE

*What do you think about desertions from the reli-
gious life, getting a dispensation, running away, etc?*

The Venerable Founder of the Oblates of Mary
Immaculate wrote to Father Martin in 1837: "We
deceive ourselves sadly if we close our eyes to this sort
of thing under the pretext that a dispensation may be
granted. We know very well indeed that a dispensation does not free the religious in conscience, unless
serious reasons, which did not exist at the time of
profession and which the religious could not foresee,
suddenly turn up and make it impossible for him to

fulfill his obligations.—And even then, the religious should receive the dispensation with regret and with a sincere desire to surmount the difficulty which prevents his remaining in the Congregation, and which evidently must not be of his own making. When the Sovereign Pontiff frees a religious from his vows, he supposes that such reasons exist, and he leaves it to the conscience of the individual to weigh their validity. In such dispensations Rome thinks first of freeing the community from members who no longer belong to it at heart; leaving the individuals to form their own conscience. . . . But if a religious by his guilty conduct brings about his expulsion, he nevertheless remains responsible before God for the violation of his obligations."

Take the case of a religious who, by negligence and laxity, falls from his vocation and asks to be freed from his vows. The dispensation is granted by the Church. It is canonically valid, of course. Yes, he is considered by the Church as freed from his vows. There is no need for him to worry if serious reasons, which did not exist at the time of his profession and which he could not foresee, turned up and made it impossible for him to fulfill his obligations. To the Pope were addressed the words: "Whatsoever thou shalt loose on earth shall be loosed also in heaven."

But suppose the religious by his guilty conduct brings about his expulsion? Does he not remain responsible before God for the violation of his obligations? Has God freed him from his oaths in conscience? Can he be sure that God has given him back the freedom he asks? Such a one has reason for worry. God is good and merciful—but also just and holy. *Nolite errare, Deus non irridetur* ("Be not deceived, God is not mocked") (Gal. 6:7).

What should be the attitude of a religious as regards his own and other religious communities?

Every religious should hold his own community in highest esteem because through it he receives the means that enable him to merit ever more abundant grace, even to reach the perfection of divine charity. But perhaps it would be better to revert to the feminine gender.

We just said that first of all a Sister should hold her own community in highest esteem, because it has done so much for her. That should be the primary attitude.

In the second place, since she was enrolled in her own particular community, not by chance, but by the loving designs of Divine Providence, she should be on her guard against letting herself be caught by those illusions and cunning temptations of the devil that tell her to change to some other community under pretext of higher perfection or the false notion that she can do more for the glory of God and the salvation of souls in such and such an order, where she will be duly appreciated, where her talents can be put to the best use, and so on. Such a change, frowned upon by the Church in many cases, is always fraught with danger and frequently results in the loss of the religious life itself. Let every Sister remember that the order she joined has stamped upon her its own special spirit, so much so that she cannot eradicate it, no matter where she goes, and will always, except in certain unusual cases, be homesick for the loving mother that brought her up—her own community.

In the third place, while loving her own community as the mother of her soul, she should not let herself disesteem even in the slightest way other orders or congregations or states of life. And, of course, with the greatest care she will refrain from any comparisons that would betray dislike, or contempt, or narrowness, or exclusiveness. All orders are wonderful, but hers is the most wonderful of all. Deep in her heart she knows this. But she is not given to praising what is hers, but to the generous praise of others.

I have doubts about my vocation as a religious. What should I do?

So many religious in our day ask for dispensations even from perpetual vows or, worse, simply leave, throwing the treasure of their vocation lightly overboard. Leaders in the spiritual and religious life tell us that "the religious life in our country is on the decline," that defections from the ranks of our religious are alarmingly increasing.

Let all religious beware of the great evil of seeking a dispensation from the vows they have made. All should ponder well these words of the Very Reverend Frederick T. Hoeger, C.S.Sp.:

"Are we treating God with the confidence He deserves, if we allow our spiritual life to be constantly disturbed about vocation after we have been led into it by the ordinary monitors of His divine Providence —prayer and the advice of His representatives, such as confessor, director or superior? If God has provided the wherewithal to make pins and needles for the conveniences of civilized life, who can doubt that the ordinary dispositions of His divine Providence provide the clue to His plan in regard to our lives? In the momentous decisions regarding sacred vocations as well as profane avocations, good parents and earnest religious too often weigh the signs of divine Prov-

idence in the balance with human prudence and ex-
pediency and then throw the weight of decision on the
side of the latter. They fear to trust the fatherly care
of God. They allow the devil, by means of disturbing
doubts about vocation, to destroy the peace and happiness of years, to turn hour after hour of prayer and
meditation into torture, to make of retreats in preparation for renewal of vows a veritable nightmare.
How much happier, more fruitful and more virtuous
the lives of all religious would be, if the doubting
Thomases were to cast aside with the help of God all
doubts and waverings about vocation, and cry out with
the apostle, 'I can do all things in him who strengthens
me' (Phil. 4:13)! Alas, so many children have been
taught to say the 'Our Father,' yet so few have learned
to pray the 'Our Father' with the implied worship,
fidelity and confidence in His divine plans. The in-
spired Wise Man tells us, 'There is no other God but
thou, who hast care of all' (Wis. 12:13)."

In this connection it may be well for all to remember that nervous, harassed, overburdened Sisters, bearing all the pressures of modern times, with too heavy
schedules, with little or no background, without time
to prepare even their daily work, may be martyrs, may
be working themselves into early graves. But they are
not the kind of martyrs modern girls wish to imitate.
Here is a kind of a vicious circle. If we do not have
enough Sisters to go around, and that is now the case,
we overburden those we do have. If we overburden
them, we not only deprive them of the peace and joy
which they have a right to expect in the religious
life, but we deter girls from following in their foot-
steps—or if they begin to follow, they soon fall by the
wayside. And if vocations fall off, we have fewer Sisters than ever to do the work.

In a fit of rebellion I asked for a dispensation from my religious vows. Now I am filled with deep regret. The dispensation has not yet come. How can I recall my request?

The Sacred Congregation of Religious was asked whether a religious who has obtained an indult of secularization or a dispensation from simple vows can refuse to accept the indult or the dispensation when he receives notice of it from the local superior, although the general superior has already issued in writing, in accordance with c. 56, the decree executing the rescript.

The reply was in the affirmative (yes, the religious could refuse to accept it), provided superiors have not grave reasons to the contrary, in which case they should refer the matter to the Sacred Congregation. (A.A.S. XIV (1922), 501)

This means that the dispensation will go into effect only after you, who asked for it, accept it. Therefore, if you regret your request and refuse to take advantage of the dispensation, or tell your superior at the moment when the dispensation is communicated to you that you do not accept it, you remain bound by your vows and a member of the institute.

Ordinarily the superiors will be as happy about your refusal to accept as you are. They realize that in a thoughtless moment you made the greatest mistake of your life and are glad you have come to your senses before it is too late.

But it may be that your superiors have grave reasons for wishing or desiring your departure from the institute because of your inconstancy, your contempt of the rules, the bad example you have been giving, your hysteria, or what have you. In that case they should refer the matter to the Sacred Congregation.

Three of our Sisters left the order recently, one at the expiration of temporal vows and the other two with a dispensation from perpetual vows. What do you think of this evil of seeking a dispensation from religious vows?

Through prayer and a faithful observance of the rules, by excelling in religious observance, the members of an order should seek to avoid the deplorable evil of seeking a dispensation from their religious vows. It is a great evil. Often enough those who seek a dispensation do not do so because they were crossed in anything, nor because they were not treated well. They are permitted to do as they please, lest they become too dissatisfied. So it is easy to see that an easy life in religion does not guarantee perseverance. When religious give themselves up to a worldly spirit for some years, discarding the habit is an easy matter.

Some religious seem to think that quitting the religious life regardless of all vows, simply applying for a dispensation, means nothing worse than a mere change in their personal plans and aspirations. In this thought they may be confirmed by the fact that many others have stepped out without more ado. A dispensation was asked for; it was granted; they were free to go. They fail to take into consideration that the Church indeed grants a dispensation, but takes it for granted that there was a very serious reason, that it was perhaps a case of being advised to leave the order because, for example, a certain individual was abnormally nervous, a stumbling block to the community. Such a counsel to depart may be given by the superiors or by the confessor or the spiritual director. Then it is better to go and there need be no qualms of conscience because of the step taken.

Every desertion from the religious life, except in cases such as those just mentioned, is saddening and a cause of more or less unhappiness for the poor soul that broke its covenant with God. The training each one receives in the religious life seems to stamp the soul with a sort of indelible mark. One is never the same afterwards, no matter where one goes, no matter what one does. How many have left and have quickly repented and have tried in vain to come back to the mother that nurtured them in religion—and have then been obliged to resign themselves to the inevitable separation from their institute. "Though hundreds of miles from the mother house, I would come back on my knees to that hallowed place if only you would permit me to enter again!" "I have been out many years now, and I have been happily married and have been living a good life, but I hope I did not make too big a mistake when I left," wrote another, wistfully. It seems that they never forget.

No wonder. God is infinite in holiness and infinite in majesty; and those who made perpetual profession consecrated themselves to Him forever. They of their own free will swore eternal fidelity to God who is omnipotent and worthy of limitless love. If lukewarm, light-minded religious revoke this consecration without a very serious reason, without the advice of those who take the place of God in their regard, it may well be a betrayal, the consequences of which are sad and fatal. "Be not deceived," we read in Holy Writ, "God is not mocked."

However, we must bear in mind that if religious leave after the expiration of temporary vows, there can be no reproaches. It is their right, often their duty and the exercise of good common sense: they see they are not fit, that they cannot take it. But if they leave when their confessors and superiors are convinced that they are called, they voluntarily disregard the holy will of God. They may have a hard time of it elsewhere then.

In a circular letter (May 31, 1944) of the Most Reverend Anthime Desnoyers, O.M.I., Vicar General, we read, among other things: "We may well ask ourselves of what value a dispensation granted to a religious who by negligence and laxity falls from his vocation and asks to be freed from his vows. Undoubtedly from the canonical point of view the dispensation is valid, and the beneficiary of the indult is considered by the Church to be freed from his obligations. But has God freed him from his promises and his oaths in conscience? In each of his acts, as in the whole series of his shortcomings which led to the loss of his vocation, the unfaithful religious broke one by one the bonds that he had promised and sworn to God to keep. Can we believe that at a given moment he had a just motive to go back on his promises and his oaths? And how can he be sure that God has given back to him the freedom which he asks? We have certainly reason to worry in trying to answer that question. God in His goodness is clement and merciful, and does not ask the impossible. But He is also infinitely just and holy, and He does not brook treating His Divine Majesty with levity, by unfaithfulness to the sacred promises solemnly contracted with Him. *Nolite errare, Deus non irridetur* (Gal. 6:7)."

If against the advice of confessor and/or superiors you have applied for a dispensation from your vows and are now sorry that you did so, then simply refuse to accept the dispensation when the official document comes. The whole thing will then become null and void and you remain true to the Savior in the religious life. And you will probably never begin the process again.

Do you think the religious habit is a handicap, is too cumbersome, impractical, unhealthful, and all that—in hot weather, for instance?

Religious do not seem to think so, no more than a soldier thinks that of a uniform and a gun, which he gets on entering the army. When visiting the Naval Academy at Annapolis one time with some Sisters who wished to see the place, we were much impressed by the uniform of the cadets, what a distinctive air it gave them, how it added to their poise and polish. Nor could we help noting the courteous deference which the cadets paid to the Sisters because of *their* uniform. "No lay person, no matter how mature, well prepared, or generous in devotion, can remotely approach the influence of the youngest, least experienced member of a community garbed in the distinctive habit of her Order." So wrote a laywoman in *America*.

Apropos of this is the story of a lay catechist who was taking the place of a Sister. After she had given a perfect instruction to the children, she had to hear their instinctive, eager, sincere query: "Will *Sister* be back next week?"

Sisters do not question the usefulness of the holy habit, as they lovingly call it, which they so longed to receive. They seldom complain, even when uncomfortably conscious of the skirts that almost touch the ground, starched collars, confining headdress. "How can she endure it?" people ask. "Just look at those yards of material!" "Isn't it wasteful?" "How can she stand that confining band about her head, that unwieldly bonnet?" "How can she endure it in this temperature?" But Sisters in a matter-of-fact manner accept the religious habit as a thing inseparable from the religious life. They have a saving sense of humor too. And when those questions are asked by a lady "much befurred as to the neck and much bare as to the legs" or by one whose high heels make her a walking representation of the leaning tower of Pisa or by one who has on her head a caricature of a hat, the Sisters simply smile.

It is true that Pope Pius XII in his address to 700 Mothers General and other Sisters in Rome on September 15, 1952, said: "Here are Our recommendations. With vocations in their present critical state, see to it that the religious habits, the manner of life, or the asceticism of your religious families do not form a barrier or a cause of failure in vocations. We speak of certain usages which, while they once had meaning in another cultural milieu, are meaningless today, and in which a truly good and courageous girl would find only obstacles to her vocation. In Our statement of last year We gave various examples of this. To repeat briefly on the question of clothing: the religious habit must always express consecration to Christ; that is what everyone expects and desires. But the habit should also conform to modern demands and correspond to the needs of hygiene. We could not fail to express Our satisfaction when, in the course of the year, We saw that some congregations had already put some of these ideas into practice. In a word, in these things that are not essential, adapt yourselves as far as reason and well-ordered charity advise."

It is, therefore, quite true that the Holy Father recommended modifications in the religious habit when this is necessary for the better accomplishment

of the work of the institute or is detrimental to vocations. Since then a number of other orders have sensibly altered the religious habits. It seems that Rome
will readily grant this permission if the request is
sponsored by the majority of the members of an institute and if the change can be made without the loss
of harmony. The main thing is to keep peace in the
religious family.

It is anyone's guess how many institutes will find a
majority who wish to modify the habit and will then
proceed to do so without loss of harmony. After all,
most religious love the habit in which they were
clothed on one memorable day and think that it is
the best in the world, all things to the contrary notwithstanding. Which reminds us of an observation
made by an American delegate to the first International Congress of Mothers General mentioned
above. "Looking at the habits that garb some of
these dear, good religious, we can't wonder that the
Holy Father of us all would like to see us clad in less
grotesque and more unostentatious dress! Ours is
surely the simplest here." Then she added: "But it
may be that everyone else thinks the same of hers!"

III

RELIGIOUS DISCIPLINE

How about the use of the telephone, the radio, and television by religious?

In a recent (1953) approval of the constitutions of a congregation of Sisters, the Holy See inserted the article: "The use of the telephone and radio is to be regulated by the superior." In its reply to the quinquennial report of a congregation of the same type the Holy See stated: "Listening to the radio in private does not appear becoming; therefore, it would be better to forbid it."

From this we may gather that local superiors may make any regulations and give any permissions which

they deem prudent in the Lord as regards the use of
the telephone. Charity, business, office work, associa-
tion with externs in general, family circumstances,
even custom, as in the case of telephones connecting
various rooms or sections of the house, will determine
what permissions are to be given. Superiors should be
watchful lest abuses creep in.

Religious may have radios or television sets in the
community room (unless expressly forbidden by the
respective superiors or by ordinances) for general use
and for religious, cultural, and recreational programs.
When they are used for recreation, the programs
should be suitable, and other provision must be made
for those who do not wish to listen or to look. For special late programs, as is evident, special permission
must be obtained for each program, the strictest silence
must be observed, and all care must be taken that
others in the house are not disturbed by programs.

At least one religious order that we know of has an
ordinance to the effect that no one may have a radio
without special permission of the higher superior (nor
a camera) and that no one may use the community
radio without the permission of the local superior.
The same applies with greater force to television.

All of this goes to show that the Holy See and the
religious orders are gravely concerned about the use
of these modern inventions in monasteries and convents. Good as they may be in certain ways, they can
be utterly destructive of the religious spirit. It is
bringing the world, which in the noble generosity of
their hearts the religious left, right into the convent.
And the words of the Savior may apply: "The last
state of this person is worse than the first."

What Pope Pius XII said of the movies seems to
apply also and even more to television: "Even though

one must fully acknowledge the technical and artistic importance of the moving picture, yet the unilateral influence that it has on man, and especially on youth, with its almost purely visual action, brings with it such a degree of danger of intellectual decadence that moving pictures are beginning to be considered a danger for the whole population."

What should the prescribed recreation in the religious life be like?

The best kind of recreation is made up of mild forms of amusement and light conversation. It is not a reading period. During this time religious should give all their attention, not to papers and magazines, not to radio or television, but to one another. This is the time to get acquainted with one another and to practice mutual charity in small talk that is free from all detraction, back-biting, talebearing, criticism. If we do not follow the advice of St. Benedict, who would banish from conversation all words that are intended merely to cause laughter, we should at least follow the admonition of St. Paul and avoid "foolish talking, or scurrility, which is to no purpose."

But, while avoiding levity, we must not go to the other extreme of being morose or melancholy. Such taciturn or gloomy characters should try to join in pleasant conversation. For them silence in recreation is not a virtue, but an imperfection. They must snap out of that moodiness, discontent, lack of joy in the Lord. Beware of the discontented nun! "My chief fear," writes St. Theresa, "is lest they, the Sisters, should lose the spirit of joy by which the Lord leads them; for I know what a discontented nun is."

Of this conversation Father Green, O.S.B., says: "Conversation at recreation should exclude levity and matters that would offend charity, also purely secular follies and scandals. Apart from these, fitting topics include a wide range of human activities, social, religious, and political. But matters of the spiritual life should generally not be discussed; they are too serious and too sacred for conversation. Moreover, the purpose of recreation is to relieve the strain upon the mind. We do not mean that we ought to be untrue to our spiritual purpose. Rather the contrary, as we learn from an incident related of the Apostle St. John. It is said that he used to amuse himself with a tame partridge at times. One day a hunter saw the saint thus occupied, and thought it strange that one so holy should descend to such trifles. St. John, reading his thoughts, asked him why he had unstrung his bow. The hunter replied that, if he did not loosen the strings at times, the bow would lose its elasticity. Then St. John told him kindly, that it was to relieve the strain of his mind that he amused himself with the partridge, so that his mind would always retain its alacrity in divine contemplation. It is for that end that religious partake of recreation."

In recreation, study and master your nature. Excite it nobly when it is inclined to moroseness. Hold it in check when it would be carried away by impetuosity. Do not let it yield to feelings of attraction to one or aversion to another. Keep the tongue well under control as regards rash judgments. But let recreation be a real relaxation none the less. Be cheerful with a holy liberty and genuine restraint.

Could you give me some more pointers for community recreation?

Remember that recreation is a community exercise and all are obliged to assist at it, to be present and to take part in it, unless detained by duties done out of obedience, and even then they should join the community as soon as they can get away from such duties. It is a time of relaxation for mind and body, a time in which to foster and preserve among the members of the community a fraternal spirit of union and charity.

Think before each recreation of how you are going to spend it. Resolve to be meek, cheerful, charitable; think how you will avoid faults of speech, dissipation, giddiness, and all that, by being mindful of the presence of God.

Look out for particular friendships and antipathies. Be willing to walk, to talk, to play with all without distinction. St. John Berchmans said: "I will love all my brethren without distinction." And be gay, pleasant, full of kindness, sincerity, and good will. Do not be disagreeable by moodiness, sorrowful looks, affected seriousness. On the other hand, though an innocent joke may please sometimes, to crack one joke after the other and practice buffoonery, makes one tedious and tiresome and a bore to others. If anyone tells a joke at your expense, take it in good part. Look pleasant, please!

Don't speak much of self, unless, for example, you have been away and have experiences to tell which you know others are waiting to hear and will be grateful for.

Furthermore, as regards speech, do not speak of the faults or defects of others—of bodily wants, such as eating or drinking—of the vanities and pleasures of the world—of anything disedifying that may have happened in the house.

Avoid expressions of double meaning—of contempt —of vanity—of ridicule or mockery. Be a model of religious and social virtues. Do nothing contrary to good manners.

Don't hurt the feelings of others by revealing their faults or weaknesses or peculiarities—by ridicule—by mockery—by nicknames—by lording it over others—by quarreling (if you *must* prove a point, do it quietly and gently)—by boasting—by heatedly and stubbornly adhering to your own opinion—by using slang or incorrect language—by being noisy and boisterous—by interrupting another—by playing roughly, in a way contrary to religious gravity—by speaking or laughing too loud. And whatever you do, please don't hurt the feelings of others by fault-finding and criticizing: sensitive souls are doubly hurt by such a manifestation of an uncharitable character.

How about games? Try to take a lively interest in customary games. But be careful not to show too much attachment for play. Cards, for example, can so captivate you that other members of the community wish deep down in their hearts that they were playing cards, in order to get *such* love and attention from you. The same may be said about newspapers and magazines. How pleased and flattered many religious would be if in recreation they got the attention those "rags" get!

In the lives of the saints we sometimes read about penitential instruments, like the hair shirt, the discipline, steel chains. Are such things used in our day by those who want to do more than ordinary penance for their sins and the sins of the world?

Yes: penitential instruments such as you mention are still used—to a greater extent, indeed, than many people think. Of the items mentioned we are inclined to think that the hair cincture should become the most popular (?). It is a band of hair cloth from three to six inches wide to be put around the waist. It can do no physical harm.

Apropos of this, the following interesting communication may be, if not enlightening, at least interesting:

Do *you* wear a hair shirt? No? Then, perhaps, the very thought of any one doing so strikes you as rather medieval, if not actually fanatical. I must confess that was the way I felt until recently.

Now I think that wearing a hair shirt is a most practical means of doing penance.

From Biblical times men and women have worn hair cloth in order to do penance and to make reparation. Since the beginning of the Christian era both religious and lay men and women, in every century, have worn hair cloth. Far from being unusual, it has been almost the common thing to do for those who wished to advance in perfection. Although it used to be done publicly, it is now done in extreme privacy. And that is as it should be in this day and age. The fact that one is wearing a hair shirt should be known only to one's confessor and spiritual director.

For some time I had been thinking of emulating the saints, although a natural reticence kept me from mentioning it even to my confessor. Then, quite providentially, a Father asked me point-blank if I had ever seen a hair shirt. When I admitted that I had not, he took something out of his desk drawer that resembled a piece of gunny sack and handed it to me.

"That's a hair shirt, Brother," he said.

I unrolled the object and examined it with deep interest. I judged it to be about two and one half feet long, and perhaps a foot wide. In the center there was a hole about ten inches long by seven or eight inches wide. From each corner extended a narrow cotton ribbon some six inches or so in length. Interwoven in the coarse material were innumerable long hairs the ends of which stuck out in every direction.

"Those mean-looking hairs," Father explained, "are sterilized horsehair, so there is no danger of infection."

"So this is a hair shirt," I said musingly.

"Well, it's one type. There are other models, but this one is as good as any . . . try it on!" Father urged.

I slipped it over my head and tried to reach the ribbons in back, but the shirt was curled up and the ribbons were out of reach. I took it off again.

"I can see that it would be rather uncomfortable," I said.

"Would you like to wear it next to your skin as an experiment?" Father asked me. He must have been reading my thoughts. I accepted the offer with alacrity.

"Wear it about an hour a day for a few days and let me know what you think of it. But wear it only in the privacy of your room of course. It isn't advisable to wear it while working."

I took the shirt to my room and that very evening prepared to put it on. I looked at it rather doubtfully. A feeling that this was all foolishness came over me. But realizing that Satan might be trying to discourage me from doing something that I knew to be good, I quickly donned the garment.

During the first fifteen minutes I found it not at all uncomfortable. "It isn't so lethal as I expected it to be," I said to myself. But then I began to feel a little discomfort; and when the hour was up, I felt a little relieved as I took it off. Not that the irritation was excessive, but I think it was simply because I was unused to such constant itching.

My skin was quite red in spots, but the itching stopped almost immediately and within an hour all the redness had gone. Frankly, I was a little disappointed because I had found the wearing of a hair shirt a very mild penance indeed.

It wasn't until I had worn it daily for several days that I realized that the irritation was progressive up to a certain point. Then I knew that wearing a hair shirt became heroic when it was worn every day, regardless of the length of the period during which it was worn. If wearing it for ten minutes caused intense distress, then certainly that was more meritorious than wearing it for several hours while feeling only a mild discomfort.

One of the most annoying things about my hair shirt is that it curls up under my habit and crawls up under my arms, creating much discomfort, but little pain. This annoying characteristic irritated me so much at first that I was on the verge of becoming angry. Soon, however, I realized how ridiculous that was. Here I wore a hair shirt for penance and because it proved to be uncomfortable in a manner different from that which I anticipated I was about to lose my temper. I could not help laughing. Now I offer up this additional discomfort, along with the itching and scratching of the horsehair.

While, I suppose, the hair shirt is worn primarily as a practical means of penance and reparation, I am convinced that it is also a real deterrent to sin. Mortifying the senses brings them under control and the wearing of a hair shirt is certainly a proper means of doing this. It cannot be called a medieval or fanatical means. If you do not believe me, try it yourself.

Thus far the communication. Needless to say, no one should make use of penitential instruments such as those mentioned in your question without permission of the confessor. It will be up to him to say for how long a time, how often, and under what conditions. It is also to one's confessor that reports should be made regarding the benefits derived from their use. Should such use prove harmful, he will prudently bid the penitent abstain from the same. No: I do not know where you can get them. I had a source; but the demand was so great that those cloistered nuns had to discontinue making them. Generally each order provides for its own members.

One time a group of novices, assembled with their mistress, were shown a collection of the various penitential instruments made by some Carmelite nuns. The Father who showed them said that most of the orders came from priests and religious. They looked so terrible that one dear young novice grew faint and, thinking discretion better than valor, sat down. Wasn't that funny?

A saving sense of humor is always in place—even when discussing a matter so seemingly horrifying as penitential instruments.

A group of young religious were discussing penances. One said: "Well, I don't know much about these penitential instruments, but any time I wanted to do penance, I was plenty satisfied with praying for a while with my arms extended." Another replied: "Sure, and *that's* not much of a penance!" "Have you tried it?" quizzed the first. "Sure I did," came the prompt answer, "and sometimes for fifteen or twenty minutes at a time." The group looked amazed (and amused), but nothing further was said. However, an older religious who had heard the conversation, cornered the brave one some time later and asked: "Look here, how do you manage to pray that long with your arms extended?" "Oh, that's easy," was the reply. "Before I go to sleep at night I lie on my back and extend my arms to pray a while. How long—why, that all depends upon how sleepy I am or how cold it is!"

Another would-be follower of the saints claimed not to be able at all to see what there was to wearing "those chain things." Said the scoffer: "Why, as soon as the chill wears off you don't know you have them on . . . they're hard on the clothes though." That last remark led to further questioning. It really *was* easy for said religious, who had blissfully worn the chains with the points turned *out*!

I find that the general tendency is to speak with bated breath about penitential instruments, as of something that might possibly disturb one's peace of mind or be injurious to one's health or even give others the impression that one wants to be a saint. Hence it is refreshing to recall how in religious communities where the use of the discipline (scourge) is a regular practice, that cat-o'-nine-tails, or less, is often found hanging on a nail in the room, back of the door or on the wardrobe cabinet, within handy reach, and is cheerfully referred to as "the fire extinguisher." This can be applied to the fires of concupiscence or of hell, or to both.

I was a bit surprised at the repercussions to my article in *Review for Religious,* issue of March, 1949, entitled "Re: Penitential Instruments." I mean the inquiries, the correspondence, that have been coming my way ever since, as though I were an expert in this particular field. Just now I received a new chain cincture, sent with a threefold purpose in view: 1. to add

to my interesting collection; 2. to ask if, in my opinion, those links should also be filed (and indeed they
should—no least wound may be caused); 3. to get my
suggestion as to what price ought to be asked for the
new commodity. All of this goes to show that you
never know what you are going to get into when you
put your pen to paper.

One religious tells me that if a religious teacher
patiently suffers contradictions, misunderstandings, if
she bears it patiently when at times she is misjudged,
even when she does what is right, she thinks it is more
meritorious before God than wearing penitential garments. Moreover, she avers, bearing with the faults
and defects and weaknesses of others, whatsoever they
may be, is not always an inconsiderable penance. She
rightly thinks that bearing with others in a spirit of
Christian charity is very pleasing to God. She goes
on to say that a religious teacher has to undergo a hard
and long struggle with herself before she learns fully
to master herself and to direct all her affections toward God. The teacher's life is a difficult one, filled
with manifold distractions. She is convinced that the
life of a religious, if she observes her constitutions
faithfully, is a cross and a martyrdom. All of this is
very true; and so are her concluding words, to the
effect that in every human life there is a Calvary and
the way leading up to it must be trod by the soul
alone.

Yet another Sister tells me, quite wisely, of course,
that corporal mortification is good in its place. But in
the case of a teaching Sister it must be practiced with
great discretion, if at all. A teacher needs strength to
do her work well. As a matter of fact, she says, a
teacher has countless opportunities to practice mortification every day when she has a class of lively and

restless youngsters before her, every one of whom seems to be wearing a hair shirt. She is of the opinion that if a teacher accepts these God-sent opportunities daily, she will practice sufficient mortification, without wearing hair shirts, chains, or taking the discipline.

Then there is the Sister who says that she learned about the penitential instruments with great joy, but that she does not think that they are very practical for most people, though she understands fully that some are called to this form of mortification. She believes that she is cross enough at times, and that wearing a hair shirt surely would not sweeten her disposition. However, just for the sake of the experience she would like to try such penitential instruments. Of course, even when using them experimentally, she would make the good intention "to make up what is lacking of the sufferings of Christ, in my flesh, for His body, which is the Church." All of this is quite sensible indeed.

Others write to the effect that they think the discipline is the most practical of all the instruments; that hair shirts and hair waists and steel chains would make one cross if one were to wear them during the day; that teaching is hard enough without wearing a hair shirt; that a teacher who remains patient in her classroom, and does her duty day after day, does all the penance she is able to perform; that, if a teacher would wear a penitential garment, it would take almost supernatural strength to be patient, kind, and devoted to her classroom interests and duties; that a teacher can radiate Christ better without going to such extremes; that, if a teacher does her duty, she will have plenty to suffer; that to face a class of children and deal with them according to the mind of Christ demands physical endurance, whereas wearing an instrument of penance seems to be robbing the body of necessary strength; that it is preferable to have and to use the perfect charity of Christ rather than to have and to use instruments of torture.

To some of these objections I could reply that, when speaking of penitential instruments, I went out of my way to stress that chains and hair shirts and hair waists should be worn for only comparatively brief periods of time and that when one is not otherwise actively engaged. I did not have in mind a religious wearing a hair shirt in the classroom, for instance. This reminds me of a Brother who came to my room sometime ago to try on the large hair shirt. Gently I put it over his shoulders, firmly I fastened it beneath his arms. Shrugging his shoulders, he said in a tone of disappointment: "Well, I thought it was worse than that. This thing wouldn't bother me much." I asked him to keep it on for an hour or two, over the bare skin, covered by his shirt and his habit, and then return and make a report. This he did. The report was to the effect that he finally had decided to wear it for one full hour, that the first fifteen minutes were not so bad, that during the second fifteen minutes the thing began to grip him with a thousand little hands, that during the third quarter of an hour he could neither work nor pray nor think of anything else except the hair shirt, and that when the last five minutes of the full hour were drawing to a close he was keeping his eyes on the clock and wondering why one short minute could be so unendurably long. From that day on he has had great respect for the hair shirt, which he dubbed "a wicked little instrument of torture."

But, to come back to my communications, there have been pros as well as cons. Thus one religious wrote: "To be perfectly frank with you, Father, I like these penitential instruments, provided they do not injure the health in any way. As long as I can remember I always wanted some kinds of instruments of penance. I always thought to myself that if I am truly zealous for the better gifts, I shall not be content with merely practicing some bodily austerities at stated times, but shall seek to practice mortification in all things and at all times—and sometimes even extraordinary corporal mortifications. Some say that we do enough penance by leaving our homes and living the religious life. This is a penance. That is true. But I often think of what a penance it was for our Lord to leave His heavenly home. And while on this earth He fasted and passed whole nights in prayer. For our sakes He endured, particularly during His bitter passion, positive pain of the flesh. He was bound, scourged, crowned with thorns, bruised, and tortured in every part of His body. The saints united their sufferings with His and chastised their bodies by means of the discipline, hair shirts, and other instruments of penance. So that is the way I feel about these penitential instruments. And now, how does a person go about getting one or more?"

Another religious wrote: "It was with great interest, Father, that I read your article on penitential instruments. I am a religious who has been in the religious life for about thirty years. Yet, sorry to say, I am none too proud of those years as far as my spiritual life is concerned. About six years ago the Lord sent me a heavy cross and thus drew me to Himself. But since then it hasn't been all fervor either. There have been ups and downs. Self-inflicted pain has often held an attraction for me. When I entered the cloister, I was disappointed to learn of the attitude that was taken

toward corporal penances. Even to speak of such
things seemed to be entirely out of order. As the years
rolled on in my religious life, I practiced mortification less and less, until six years ago when the Lord
took pity on me. I had to learn the hard way.

"Your article has given me courage, and I now
know that such practices are not altogether extinct. In
the past I have been ashamed to ask for permission to
make use of penitential instruments. No doubt this
is false shame. Now I look forward to the day when I
may make use of some of them.

"So, with the due permission for the ordering, I am
now going to order some penitential instruments from
the Carmelite Monastery. Then, of course, I will ask
permission of my confessor to use those penitential
instruments, following his instructions."

Another petitioner writes, with masculine brevity:
"I'm sending this note hoping that you have an extra
hair shirt you can let me have." Just like that! "I've
received permission from my confessor to wear a hair
shirt. May God's blessing be upon you, Father, always,
and may our Blessed Mother keep you close to Jesus!"

"I have been a religious for a long, long time now;
and for many years I have been trying hard to lead an
interior life," another writes. "For some time I have
been longing to use the discipline or to wear a chain
or hair belt; but I did not know where I could get
such things, even though I had my Spiritual Director's
permission to use them. So I was very happy to read
your article in the 'Review for Religious.' My higher
Superior said we did not need the Superior's permission for such things, as long as we have a clear understanding with a Spiritual Director. I have that and I
also have very good health." All of this is eminently
sensible.

Some comments by other religious are interesting also. One writes that he thinks my article very sensible and matter-of-fact and that he applauds my remark that "the large hair shirt is better worn over the underwear or even over the shirt." He has tried both ways as well as over the skin and finds that my "compromise manner" is very prudent and that even in this way there is real penance.

I was rather surprised when another religious informed me that the voluntary use of penitential instruments was harder in his estimation than pains sent by God in the line of sickness—even the pains of arthritis, which he knew only too well. "You just take those pains, that's all," he said. "You can't help it and so you try to grin and bear it. But it's quite a different matter when it comes to self-inflicted pain. A man doesn't like to do that. He's free—and free not to, don't you know." Be that as it may for this individual, it remains true that the three (descending) stages of mortification are 1. doing what is commanded by God's law and refraining from what is forbidden; 2. bearing with patience and resignation all the crosses and contradictions that befall us by God's providence; and 3. self-imposed practices of mortification. Nevertheless, the religious was right in what he expressed to the extent that, as Tanquerey says in *The Spiritual Life,* "it is a matter of experience that nothing is so effective in breaking down the lure to pleasure as the voluntary undertaking of some additional labor, the shouldering of some additional burden by imposing upon ourselves some positive practices of mortification."

I have a special friend in the community and am wondering whether this is a particular friendship of the wrong kind. What are the signs of a bad particular friendship?

If you must answer yes to questions like the following, then yours is indeed an imperfect friendship.

Do you barely tolerate the presence of a third person when you are conversing together, even though you may be speaking only of ordinary matters in no way secret? Have you an attitude of "We are not like the rest of men" or of "You love me and I'll love you and we'll let the rest of the world go by"? Does each one of you resent any marks of affection paid to the other by anyone else? Are you continually thinking of your friend, even when engaged in such matters of importance as studying or praying? Have you a continual desire to see your friend? Do you experience a certain restlessness of mind when your friend is absent? Do you indulge in useless conversation when your friend is present? Do you break the silence together often, even the strictest silence? Do you visit each other's room without necessity? Is there such a thing as a frequent exchange of small gifts? Are you anxiously solicitous in hiding your friend's faults, or do you find in yourself an overreadiness to excuse them? Do you fail to subordinate your friendship to the demands of common life and common charity, so that it alienates you at least a little from the rest of the community? Do the private interests of your friend take precedence over community exercises and gatherings? Do you multiply the otherwise quite legitimate external manifestations of friendship so that they are a source of even slight disedification to others? Are those manifestations no longer quite legitimate, so that there is a proximate danger of your friendship becoming carnal?

Don't you think that religious eat too fast, do too much stuffing, at the community meals, because no one wants to be last and keep the others waiting?

Yes, we do think so, in some, perhaps most communities. To the reason you adduce we would add the aggravating circumstance that Americans in general are a race of hasty eaters.

We recall reading in the rules of one religious community, rules written by St. John Eudes, that the meal should be taken without haste, so that the members may eat with ease, health, and comfort. The rule stated that the meal may be protracted up to one hour, so that all may eat in that healthful, becoming manner. We also recall how one superior general once wrote in an official communication to all the members of the order that there should be no hurry in the partaking of meals, that it is a good thing to listen for five or ten minutes more to the table reading. This superior general put his advice into practice in the motherhouse in Rome. He would not ring the bell in the refectory until at least thirty minutes had passed, but would sit, watch in hand, and just wait, even if all were finished. It was his way of letting them all know that there was no need to hurry, that they might as well eat leisurely, since they would have to sit at table just so long anyway. It would be good if all superiors would make it a point to do something like that and also to make it their practice to be the last ones to finish eating.

In "The Watches of the Passion" we read: "Were we present in the Cenacle, we should also assuredly notice how our Savior and those He has trained are not only very temperate and abstemious, but also not at all hasty or precipitate in eating and drinking; and how with great charity they prevent one another's wants, and how they are all more impressed by the holy thoughts which their Master suggests than by the courses served to them."

One should pay good attention to the table reading and try to derive from it pleasure and profit. Such attention is a manifestation of respect and gratitude toward the reader, who in turn will pay a compliment to the hearers by reading correctly, intelligently, and in a way that all can understand easily and without too much concentration. The reader who reads too fast, or who does not read loud enough, or who stumbles over words and phrases and repeats them, or who even mispronounces words, either is not listened to by those who are busy with the necessary chore of eating or positively shows that he does not esteem as he should the select audience he is privileged to address.

IV

SUPERIORS

*Don't you think we ought to be more democratic in
this country and treat our superiors in an open and
jovial way and not be so servile?*

Be open, frank, cordial, smiling, friendly, in all
sincerity of heart toward your superiors always; do not
be servile, cringing, cold, reserved, guarded. Only too
often superiors have to handle their subjects with silk
gloves—and even then they, despite all caution, touch
them the wrong way, little realizing how very sensitive
dust can be!

We cannot be too democratic in the good way sug-

gested by the first words of the above paragraph. It
often seems to us that the apostles were democratic in
that way in the community which they formed around
the Divine Savior. But how reverent they were toward
Him at the same time! Meditate on the Gospels.

Always be very reverent toward your superiors, remembering that they take the place of Christ. See
Jesus in them and reverence and obey them as *Him.*
What examples we have of this among the saints. St.
Francis Xavier, out of respect, used to get down on
his knees whenever he was writing a letter to his
superior, St. Ignatius Loyola. In some communities
subjects always speak to the superiors in their rooms
on their knees. In others all bow low to the superior
upon entering the chapel. In some orders it is prescribed that the members always ask for a blessing
when entering the room of a superior. Resolve to
reverence your superiors more. We are already too
democratic in this matter.

How would you act toward the Savior were He
visibly and in person the superior of your community?

*I wish I could be superior sometime too; it must be
nice to be over others. Don't you think so too?*

The Divine Savior died on the cross for our sanctification and salvation. Meditation on the passion
teaches us what an awful price He had to pay.
Throughout the centuries He has let millions of
martyrs suffer and die in order to bring nations to the
true Faith; for the blood of martyrs is the seed of
Christians. Among the martyrs we might count religious superiors. The Master has chosen to represent
Him in each community a special victim, the superior,
who is the medium of His communications to the rest.

It is at their cost that superiors are among us. Uneasy is the head that wears a crown. How often our heart goes out in pity to the Holy Father, to bishops, to generals of religious orders, as we recall the burdens they bear, the loneliness they must endure because of their exalted positions. And yet we know that it is not without great merit to themselves that our superiors are among us. What an opportunity, too, for practicing Christian charity by their goodness, simplicity, and loving condescension. What a chance day after day to promote the sanctification of souls and the glory of God by gently but firmly seeing to it that all the rules are observed and the spiritual exercises performed. How happy the lot of those who can thus make others happy. Yes, we think it must be nice to be over others, to be a superior, if one is a real lover of the cross of Christ, because then one is very close to Christ, so close that one can say: "With Christ I am nailed to the cross!" Only remember well that when one is a superior, one is not really over others, but under them. The Pope calls himself "the servant of the servants of God."

In almost the same breath you ask: "Is obedience of judgment really right? Putting aside a case where I merely cannot understand my superior's reason, supposing that I actually see that she is wrong, to yield to her outwardly is meritorious, but to approve of her inwardly—is not this exacting a sort of mental suicide which is absurd, immoral, impossible, unreasonable?" Suppose you were in the enviable position of the superior now. What would you expect? You who are so close to Christ on the cross and are willing to be a victim soul for the glory of God and the good of others would expect others too, in the generosity of their hearts, to embrace the folly of the cross. It is eminently reasonable for subjects to distrust their own judgment, to realize that superiors see from a height, that they have special graces and lights. Anyone who has ever been in a position of authority in a religious order knows full well that it is not at all the custom to choose the least capable and least worthy to govern.

How often we have been at prayer, resolved not to be at all wilfully distracted, and have seen something through the window that mightily attracted our gaze. We saw it; it was there; and yet we did not look. We did not look again. Our duty was just then the duty of prayer. When you see that superiors are weak and frail in commands and in themselves, simply do not look. Yours is then the duty of obedience. Such non-looking is not absurd, immoral, impossible, unreasonable.

Isn't the superior just one of us anyhow? Why stress so much the office of a superior?

Take a community of Sisters gathered in recreation, no superior present, all equals. That is today. Tomorrow comes the promulgation of an election by the higher superior and her consultors. One of the Sisters who yesterday was merely one among equals has been made superior. She is no longer just one of the community, as she was yesterday. She was invested with office according to the constitutions, which means in the name of God and of His Vicar, for the Pope is the highest superior of all religious. When so invested, something analogous to what takes place on the altar at the Consecration took place: God became truly present in your midst in the person of your superior. In both cases we have a mystery of faith to our human understanding; but in both cases the thing is a divine reality.

Remember that in a religious all virtues are united

with obedience. For a religious to do well at all times and in all things, it suffices to obey.

An obedient religious must be ready to subordinate his own likes and preferences, must be dependent as to his activities and place of residence. But there is always considerable room for initiative and freedom in doing the work assigned, since consultation with superiors about details is often simply impossible. The modern ideal of the apostolic religious is that he should "obey from within by conforming his own mind and will to that of his superior, and that he should exercise a certain independence and initiative in carrying out the work assigned."

Most superiors are kind and gentle. But sometimes one gets a superior who is cold, ungracious, exacting, or at least seems to be so. What should one do then?

Nevertheless recognize, adore, and kiss the hand of God in the hard but consecrated hand of that superior. Leavened bread is rougher than unleavened bread, and it is less white; but, once consecrated, what do these appearances matter? The crucifix on your rosary is not nearly so large as the one above the tabernacle or on the altar; and yet you show the same honor to both. Both represent the same dear Savior Who "loved me and delivered Himself for me." The superior is God's delegate in your regard; and to the lowest delegate you give the same obedience as to the one who delegates. In this case your obedience is to God Himself, the principle of all delegation.

Sometimes religious ask how superiors take the place of God, since they are chosen from among us. Monsignor Gay says, apropos of this:

"As after the consecration the whole substance of the bread is changed into the body of the Lord, who in an inexplicable manner transforms it into His own substance without using it as nourishment; so in the same manner, after their nomination, time, health, strength, life, intellect, heart, all that may be comprehended under the term of the substance of superiors, is in a manner completely absorbed by the commission they have received, by the power conferred on them, and by the charge entrusted to their keeping."

They do take the place of God. The words just quoted may well be meditated upon by all religious. Superiors will be filled with a sense of their responsibility; and those who are not superiors will breathe a prayer that they may never be called upon to bear that burden.

Since the superiors take the place of God, why does God so often leave defects unremoved in those who have authority? On the other hand, why do some superiors make so little of their authority? Do you not think they should take upon themselves more the character of God, whose place they take?

First of all, we may say without any hesitation that the faults of superiors are certainly exaggerated, just because they are superiors and have the grave duty of seeing to it that religious observance flourishes. In the performance of that duty it will be necessary for them at least occasionally to give directions, issue ordinances, correct, reprove, and even punish. Human nature being what it is, the sensitiveness of subjects will often rise up in rebellion and will magnify, at least in thought, the imperfections of the superiors.

But superiors do have defects. Why? Because to appoint a superior does not mean to work a miracle. Because defects are good for those who have them:

"Virtue is made perfect in infirmity." They promote humility, dampen exaltation. Because of the good of the subjects: to obey a defectful superior is high perfection. There would not be so much merit in obedience if you had an archangel as a superior.

The superiors on their part should realize that they take the place of God and act accordingly. Says Monsignor Gay: "No doubt superiors themselves ought to be the first to believe with a firm and practical faith in their own authority. If they are not convinced that, though nothing in themselves, they are nevertheless made divine in authority, how can they do divine work? Many fail in this duty, and hence often comes the uncertainty, weakness, and inefficiency of their rule. The faith of the preacher calls forth the faith of the hearer."

V

POVERTY

What is really the essence of the vow of poverty?

First of all, what is a vow? A vow is a deliberate, voluntary promise made to God to do something that is pleasing to Him, though there is no obligation to do it. The vow of poverty consists essentially in depriving oneself, to please God, of either the right (solemn vow) to possess or to acquire for oneself any temporal goods whatsoever, or (simple vow) the independent disposal of temporal goods or of any object having a money value. Independent disposal would be without the permission of the superior. The vow of poverty, as is evident, is the counterpart of an

inordinate pursuit of riches. By it the religious gives
up the goods of this world, the material goods, just
as by the vow of chastity he gives up the goods of the
body and by the vow of obedience that most precious
possession which is his own will.

Just what a religious renounces by his vow of
poverty cannot be told in a general reply. One must
consult the constitutions of each order or congregation in order to find out accurately the meaning and
extent of the vow made therein. It has greater or less
extent and imposes obligations more or less strict
according to the different religious institutes. It is not
always greater or less fervor which gives rise to these
differences, but rather the purposes of the institutes.

Voluntary poverty is the first of the eight beatitudes.
"Blessed are the poor in spirit, for theirs is the kingdom of heaven."

Christ counseled voluntary poverty. How impres-
sively this is brought to our minds anew when we read
of the rich young man in the Kleist-Lilly translation
of the New Testament: "If you want to be perfect,"
Jesus said to him, "go and sell all your possessions and
give the proceeds to the poor—for which you will have
an investment in heaven; then come back and be my
follower." When the young man heard the answer, he
went away with a heavy heart; for he had much
property.

Then Jesus said to his disciples: "I tell you frankly:
a rich man will find it difficult to enter the kingdom
of heaven. I repeat: it is easier for a camel to pass
through the eye of a needle than for a rich man to
enter the kingdom of God." On hearing this, the
disciples were completely bewildered. "In that case,"
they said, "who can be saved?" But Jesus looked
straight at them and said: "Where man fails, God still

avails." Here Peter took occasion to say to him: "We, you see, have given up everything and become your followers. What, then, are we to get?" Jesus said to them: "I tell you with assurance: in the final regeneration, when the Son of Man takes his seat on a throne befitting his glory, you, my followers, will, in turn, be seated on twelve thrones and have jurisdiction over the Twelve Tribes of Israel. And so in general: whoever gives up home, or brothers, or sisters, or father, or mother, or children, or lands, for the sake of my name, will receive a hundred times as much and inherit eternal life" (Matt. 19: 21-29).

What are the principal sins against the vow of poverty?

The principal sins against the vow of poverty are these:

1. Without permission of the superior to take for oneself or another an object belonging to the house.

2. Without permission to retain possession of an object, especially to keep it as if one were its real owner, as when one hides it away so that superiors may not take it. But to retain books, manuscripts, beyond the time fixed is generally not a grave fault.

3. To give or receive without permission. But in exceptional circumstances it is not forbidden to accept a thing with presumed permission with the intention of later getting authorization to keep it; and one may always presume permission to receive things for the community and in its name.

4. Without permission to buy, sell, or exchange anything belonging to the community, even in the interest of the house; and if one has permission, he may do so only under conditions prescribed by the superior.

5. Without permission to lend or borrow. This is quite evident when it comes to money, for instance. It is only a light fault if lending and borrowing, as of books, is done in the community, if that practice is forbidden; but it is no fault at all if it is a legitimate custom. In this matter one must not be squeamish or rude. If a fellow religious asks for something, we charitably suppose that he has permission or that he needs no permission to borrow because everybody does it in the community and the superiors have never objected.

6. Without permission to use an object for a purpose other than prescribed, allowing for legitimate customs or permissions rightly presumed. For example, given money for traveling, one may not use it for other purposes, but what is left over must be returned to the superior.

7. Wilfully to destroy or allow to perish articles which the religious ought to take care of, as in kitchen, store-room, wardrobe, laundry. So, too, one should take at least as good care of the articles given for personal use as one would if out in the world.

8. Without permission to take along, when changed from one house to another, more than is permitted by the lawful superior or by custom. There should be no difficulty here. It is merely a case of asking what you should or may take along.

9. Without the necessary permission to dispose of one's own goods. This means the independent administration or use of the personal goods a religious may have. The constitutions are quite detailed as regards this matter.

10. The procurator may expend only in accordance with the rule and the superior's directions.

11. Superiors may not expend the revenues of the community for things that are not necessary or of no benefit to religion.

What amount is required for a mortal sin against poverty varies greatly according to the more or less strict poverty of the community, to its plenty or want, so that it is impossible to settle upon any definite figure here. (Cf. Cotel, *Catechism of the Vows.*)

I have heard it said that for many religious the hardest thing about poverty is that one must always have permission. I suppose that refers to the humiliation of having to be dependent upon the will of the superior. How many kinds of permission are there?

Yes, a legitimate permission prevents a fault against the vow of poverty, because the religious then no longer acts as the owner of the thing in question but is only carrying out, as it were, the superior's will. It is to be noted that "a permission given without limitation of time (expressed or understood) of itself holds indefinitely, but that any permission can be revoked (suppressed) by the one who gave it, his superior, or his successor" (Cotel).

Here is an enumeration of different kinds of permission:

1. Express permission, given by word or outward sign. You ask for something and the superior grants your request.

2. Tacit permission, when silence gives consent. The superior knows what is done and cannot readily refuse. We must be careful not to extend this permission beyond all reasonable bounds. It may be taken for granted when one thing is understood in the permission or command to do something else.

3. Implicit permission: when you are given permission for a journey, you have the implied permission to make the expenditures necessary for that journey.

4. General permission: when given to several persons or for several cases. A general permission may indeed be given and is quite legitimate and often very helpful in the observance of poverty, as when one asks for permission to give little things, like holy pictures, medals, to pupils when occasion offers, and receives a supply of such articles for distribution. But general permission is illicit if it tends to the weakening of religious discipline.

5. Particular permission is that which the superior gives to one person and for one case.

6. Presumed permission is that which is supposed to exist in the will of the superior. Permission may be presumed only: a. when it cannot be asked for, b. in matters of minor importance, c. when an action cannot be deferred, d. when it is morally certain that the superior would give permission. Note well that, since the fact of acquiring the thing must be reported, this also forbids one to retain temporal goods without permission. (In case the thing accepted with presumed permission is consumed before you can get permission to keep it, like a box of candy, you no longer need to ask for permission.) You may not presume permission when in your judgment the superior *should* grant permission if asked, but in reality *would* not do so. Sometimes it is even our duty to use presumed permission, as when we know that the superior would want us to presume it, e.g., in order not to lose a good opportunity.

7. Valid permission is one which the superior has the right to grant, which right the subject ordinarily takes for granted. A permission is invalid when there

is no right to grant it on the part of the superior, over whom we are not appointed judge.

What is the difference between the vow and the virtue of poverty?

In general, and this holds for all three vows or religion, the vow is: 1. a means toward the attainment of the virtue; 2. the vow does not directly extend beyond those things which it requires under pain of sin, whereas the virtue can mount to ever higher perfection; 3. the virtue in turn is a means toward the preservation of the vow; and 4. a religious can sin against the virtue without violating the vow.

In particular, the virtue of poverty is that which inclines the heart of the religious to detach itself from affection for temporal goods. This interior detachment is the object of the first beatitude: "Blessed are the poor in spirit, for theirs is the kingdom of heaven."

A religious who has the spirit of poverty will accustom himself to regard as consecrated to God all that belongs to the community and even what is given for his own use; he will cling to nothing; he will look upon himself as a beggar living on alms; he will thus practice penance and become Christlike. Such a religious will:

1. Practice poverty in dress. Choose what is cheaper and coarser when you must select it yourself. Have nothing superfluous in your wardrobe; but remember that the notion of the superfluous, elastic and variable as it is, is determined by the purpose, constitutions, or customs of the individual religious institutes. Find no fault with what is given you. But cheapness is not synonymous with uncleanliness. Our dress must be respectable and not repulsive. Even St. Benedict re-

quires that, when religious appear in public, they should be dressed a little better than usual.

2. Practice poverty in diet. Thankfully accept what is provided. Be content with ordinary diet. Do not extort permission for delicacies. If you have this spirit, you will feel humiliated when you are obliged to be on a diet and to get better service than the others. Do not complain of incompetency of cooks, carelessness of officials, want of more tasty dishes, monotony of diet. "At one time he was a beggar; now he is a fastidious monk!" Be *moderate* in eating and drinking. Do not be wasteful of food by carelessly leaving portions on your plate to be thrown away.

3. Practice poverty in your room and furniture. Be satisfied with the place that has been assigned you. Remove everything superfluous from time to time. Let your cell be neither gorgeous nor disorderly. Practice poverty in the use of necessary things. One can be economical in the use of electric light, for instance, by using enough indeed, but switching it off when leaving the room; in the use of soap, by using up the little pieces; in the use of water, by not letting it run unnecessarily; and thus in many other things. Religious should at least be as careful of the articles given for their use as they would have been of their own goods in the world.

4. The spirit of poverty can be especially exercised by living the *common life* and avoiding its most fatal breach: "pocket money," *peculium.*

What is meant by the common life and by "pocket money," peculium?

First of all, and fundamentally, the common life means membership in a society which enjoys moral personality under a determined superior and a definite rule and dwelling together under a common roof, sharing common lodging and board with others. This is one of the elements of the religious state (canon 487).

Then the common life, which must be exactly observed by all, even in those things which pertain to food, clothing, and furniture, demands that whatever is acquired by religious must be incorporated in the goods of the house, or of the province, or of the institute, and that all money and securities shall be deposited in the common safe (canon 594).

We have translated the Latin word *peculium* as "pocket money," in the absence of anything better that we know of by way of an English rendition. But not all pocket money is *peculium*. It does not mean money which one carries on one's person, in one's pocket or purse, at least not necessarily. When a constitution says, for instance, that pocket money is absolutely forbidden in the congregation and the superiors have no power to permit or tolerate it, this does not mean the money given to go on a journey.

In *Review for Religious*, Vol. 7, p. 33, Father Adam C. Ellis, S.J., has an excellent article entitled "Common Life and Peculium," in which he thus defines peculium:

"For practical purposes we may define peculium as a small sum of money (or its equivalent) *distinct from the common fund*, which is given to an *individual* religious *to keep* for his *personal* use, and which is something *over and above* what is *required* for his *immediate* needs."

Every word of this definition must be well weighed. The definition is carefully explained in the article mentioned. Let us simply say that peculium means "a sum of money coming either from the possessions of the religious or by way of gifts received from relatives, for instance, the free use of which money the superior consents to leave to the religious. This abuse, which leads to the ruin of the spirit of poverty, is also most harmful to fraternal union and to edification. It is even against the vow if the superior renounces the right to revoke the permission, or if he gives a permission which is invalid and contrary to the constitutions" (Cotel).

The best thing for a religious to do is to ask for whatever money he needs as occasion arises, to get it from the common fund through the superior or procurator, to keep a careful account of all the expenses made, and then on his return, as soon as possible, preferably on the same day, to hand in to the superior an account of the receipts and expenses together with the balance.

Again, everything the religious gets should be handed over as soon as possible to the superior, to become a part of the common fund. Best thing is not to say, for example, "I just received five dollars from a relative; may I use it for this or that?" but simply hand it in and then later come and ask for what is needed for immediate use from the common fund, without reference to the five dollars now absorbed therein.

What are the different degrees in the practice of poverty?

The degrees in the exterior practice of poverty may be given as follows:

1. The first degree of poverty requires that the religious accept, retain, or dispose of nothing without due permission, and that he keep for his private use nothing that is not necessary. It is really to renounce all temporal goods and to dispose of nothing inde-

pendently of the superior. This is even the matter of the vow.

2. The second degree requires that the religious should not have superfluous things. He should not find fault with the economy of the superior, should not secretly procure delicacies, finer clothes, should not make his room a storehouse of curiosities, pictures, and whatnots. But because this is already implied in the first degree, he should also cheerfully bear the privations and hardships inseparably connected with genuine poverty, be content with what is necessary, and put aside all affection for temporal goods and the ease they bring with them.

3. The third degree consists in not only patiently bearing the hardships of poverty but even seeking them. Seek the worst things in the community and accept such as one's part, in what concerns dwelling, clothing. Seek occasions of practicing religious poverty.

4. The fourth degree is to love to be in want, even sometimes of what is necessary, with prudence and without danger to health, to be more like the Savior in His poverty.

Briefly: always permission; nothing superfluous; no attachment to things.

What is the amount required for a mortal sin against the vow of poverty?

This is a difficult question to answer. Generally speaking, the amount is the same as that required for a mortal sin against the seventh commandment of God. Serious matter varies a great deal according to the more or less strict poverty professed by the various institutes, as well as according to the plenty or want of the community, not to mention the economic conditions of time and place, the value of money, the daily wage. In some institutes the constitutions, or the accepted commentary on the constitutions, settles the problem by determining that a certain sum constitutes a serious violation of the vow of poverty. For example, if a given institute were to state in its constitutions that ten dollars is a grave matter, the religious of the institute would be understood to bind themselves in accordance with this norm.

Opinions of theologians differ very much in this matter and there are many controverted points. From the various authors we may gather that if the community against which the injustice is perpetrated is small and poor, so that about six dollars would represent its daily income, the religious would sin mortally by depriving the community of double that amount, twelve dollars, twice the relatively grave sum because it is taken from the religious family, who may be presumed to be "unreasonably unwilling." But if the expression just used is not understood, it may be explained by saying that in this case the goods of the community are in some sense destined for the use of the religious. However, if the religious who is offending against the vow of poverty is a member of a large and financially stable community, the sum needed for a serious violation would be much greater; unless the institute makes it clear that the relative norm is to be applied, the violation of poverty would be estimated according to the absolute norm of injustice, which would be about 35 dollars in normally good times, and perhaps 50 to 75 dollars at the present time. But the present time is very variable, even in our country. As we write this, we are in an era of unprecedented prosperity. Our standard of living is the highest of any country in the world. God has made us the stewards of His wealth, that we may give generously in His name to less fortunate peoples. But wars, depressions, catastrophes of various kinds have a way of quickly changing things.

Note that the relative norm is based upon the financial condition of the individual or group that is the victim of the injustice and is the average day's pay of the victim in question, whereas the absolute norm is the ceiling beyond which no one may go without committing a mortal sin, even though the victim be very wealthy. The absolute norm is used only in those cases in which the person injured has a daily income equal to or more than that sum. Such would be, for example, a large and prosperous community.

This should be enough. We need not enter into all kinds of distinctions here. Best thing for religious to remember is that, though an amount of a few dollars would not constitute a mortal sin, he should not be thinking of avoiding mortal sin, but all sin against poverty, by simply having permission for everything.

From time to time I am troubled when I read or hear in conference that religious who offend against the vow of poverty may also have to make restitution. How can one do that?

In *Catechism of the Vows* by Cotel-Jombart, twenty-eighth edition (1924), no. 61, the question is asked: "In violating his vow, cannot a religious also sin against justice and consequently be obliged to restitution?"

The answer is there given: "Yes, undoubtedly, any theft and any culpable damage done by a religious against his neighbor or the community is against *justice,* and then he is obliged to *restitution,* even toward the community. He must therefore make compensation for the injustice he has done the house, either from his personal goods, or by living more economically, or by extra work if he is capable of it, or he may obtain a condonation from superiors."

In *Review for Religious*, Vol. IV, p. 205, there is the question: "If a religious has *unjustly* disposed of money belonging to his institute, is he obliged to make restitution?"

The answer is then given: "If he has property of his own, he is certainly obliged to recompense the institute from his own funds. For determining the method of making such restitution, he should consult a confessor. If he has no property, he may generally consider himself as excused from the obligation of making restitution until such time as he would become the possessor of property. This would very likely mean that in many cases the religious would be perpetually excused from making restitution to the institute; but it seems to be the most practicable solution to the case. It is sometimes suggested that the religious should get a condonation from a superior (provided the superior has the power to give a condonation), but this solution is open to the danger of self-revelation, and we see no solid reason for calling it obligatory. It is also suggested that the religious can make restitution by economizing; but this suggestion seems to overlook the fact that a religious is not entitled to superfluities. He is supposed to lead a frugal life, and he could hardly be obliged to deprive himself in any notable way of the things that pertain to such a life."

In the supposition that a religious who has, let us say, accepted from a relative and spent without permission the sum of one hundred dollars, thus unjustly disposing of that amount given, it is, practically speaking, impossible for him to make restitution even if

he has property, and this because of the danger of
self-revelation and the violation of the secrecy of the
confessional and also, and especially, because it is forbidden to the professed of simple vows in religious
congregations (c. 583) to abdicate gratuitously the
dominion over their property by a voluntary deed of
conveyance, or to change the will they have made before their profession. To give to the order the sum of
one hundred dollars in any way from his property
would either be forbidden or would be so circumstan-
tial as to excuse from the restitution on the ground of
continuing moral impossibility.

This being so, we must have recourse to reasons that
excuse from restitution. In almost all cases we could
say that a religious is excused from restitution to the
community because of a physical impossibility to
restore; and this impossibility is permanent.

Likewise a moral impossibility excuses the religious,
and that permanently also, because of the genuine
inconvenience which the restitution would entail, for
example, the one restoring would certainly have to
suffer in good name because of the concomitant self-
revelation.

So, too, in this case, the poverty of the religious
debtor excuses him because he would be bound to
restore only to the poor or to pious causes, i.e., to his
community.

Finally, condonation excuses the religious from
restitution, whether it is express, tacit, or reasonably
presumed. Ordinarily presumptions must be cau-
tiously used and only after advice sought from a
prudent confessor; but in this case it may be taken for
granted.

Express condonation is had when the creditor, in
a religious community the legitimate superior, is

asked by the debtor or by another, e.g., the confessor, at the debtor's request, to remit the debt, and then does actually remit it.

A tacit condonation is had, for instance, when the religious approaches the superior and is about to tell the embarrassing tale and he dismisses the whole matter with a wave of the hand and bids the religious say no more.

A presumed condonation is had when one may prudently judge that the creditor, if asked by the debtor or by some one else in his name, e.g., the confessor, would generously forgive the debt.

A religious may quite properly presume such a condonation.

Why is the lighting so poor in many of our convent chapels? It seems that so many religious ruin their eyes by reading in the semidarkness.

Let us comment on this with a bit of the saving sense of humor. We have often noticed Sisters peering painfully, or straining to see, as they knelt or sat in the chapel with office book or meditation manual. We could not help noting that the lighting in the chapel was manifestly inadequate. The fixtures were fancy indeed; but any good gadget for determining whether the lighting in a given place is sufficiently strong for reading would have given a wholly negative reading. And yet the Sisters have to use their missals. At stated times they have to assemble in the chapel to recite the office. They come to practice their own private devotions during free time. And over and over again the light is too poor, or it is not turned on at all.

We wonder what is the reason for all this poor lighting. Is it the practice of poverty? Is it because they must be saving and hold down the light bill?

But eye strain gradually leads to visits to the eye specialist, the fitting of glasses, and thereupon periodical visits to that specialist to have the glasses changed from year to year or from time to time, as the case may be. Every such visit means expenditure. A bit of reflection and a juggling of figures might reveal that, far from being poverty, it is an offense against poverty, inasmuch as the care of the eyes of a given community costs much more in the long run than would better, scientifically correct, and sufficient lighting. It seems to be yet another case of being penny wise and pound foolish. It is to be noted, too, that many chapels are so dark, because of the stained glass windows, or because it is a dreary day, or because a storm is brewing, that not only in the morning and evening and at night, but also during the day, light sufficient to avoid all eye strain should be turned on.

When all is said, no matter how high the light bill may be, up to now one could always buy light. But one cannot buy eyes. They are a precious gift of God. The best one can do if one squanders that gift is to go through life with crutches—the bothersome crutches that are called glasses.

To the objection that, even with the best of lighting at all times, many will have to have recourse to glasses sooner or later, we reply that this is true enough, but that, while we must accept what cannot be helped, such spectacles are not to be multiplied without necessity.

To sum up: wherever this is a problem, lower your lights, increase your fixtures, augment your watts— and use generously. And superiors should let it be known in the community that everyone should turn on the light as needed, that no one need have any scruples on that score.

All this reminds us of the religious who were taught, through a misplaced stress on the observance of poverty, to use a common tooth brush and, later, an individual piece of cloth wherewith to cleanse the teeth, grew up practicing economy by neglecting their teeth, and years later caused the superior to groan in spirit: "Why, almost all the earnings of the combined community go to pay dentist bills!"

It sometimes seems that conditions in our time and country make necessary certain adaptations as regards the observance of religious poverty. How far may one go in such adaptations?

Again we must bear in mind that adaptation is not mitigation. As Pope Pius XII said when speaking to religious: "The unique path to perfection is seen to be in the denial of self for the love of Christ. The changing times in no way effect this fundamental truth." Referring to subjects, he said to superiors: "Be generous in giving them all they need, especially where books are concerned." And again: "When it comes to technical improvements . . . they should make equal progress with others, nay, surpass them." Strange as it may seem, the religious life may even decline through too great poverty, inasmuch as religious in order to get what they must have to do their work turn to relatives and friends, to the detriment of the common life.

By all means let us always preserve the spirit of poverty. Abbot Butler says: "The spirit of poverty demands that in a Benedictine monastery the conditions of life in regard to food, clothing, furniture, and the personal comforts of life, ought to be on a distinctly simpler and more frugal scale than the majority of monks would have had if they had remained in the world." And surely that much applies to all religious, at least that much.

The world around us always wants more and more earthly goods. The standard of living rises higher and higher. All this should put us on our guard, since the spirit of the world threatens to infect religious, since it is opposed to the religious spirit, since self-indulgence never lacks excuses.

We should be truly lovers of poverty as regards the common life, clothing, food, and personal comforts. As Father Creusen says, religious of today also "must renounce the world—its ease, its dissipation, its spirit of independence, and of criticism." We fail as religious by easy surrender to soft living and modern comforts.

Yet we may use present-day comforts and conveniences as a means to an end. We can employ them in the service of God, for His greater honor and glory. Creatures are good when so employed; when employed for any other purpose, they are bad. We should pray that "we may so use the things of time as not to lose those of eternity." We should use gratefully the things that enable us to have more time for prayer, study, reading, works of the ministry, charitable service, and all that leads to more perfect union with God. Here we might mention modern equipment, labor-saving devices, the typewriter, and such like things. Often, too, private rooms for study and rest, more comfortable beds, convenient use of the bath, sufficient heating, and suitable changes of clothing will enable religious to promote still more the glory of God and the salvation of souls.

But often, like St. Aloysius, they should ask themselves: *Quid hoc ad aeternitatem?* (Of what value is this for eternity?) And they should be spiritually alert as regards things like modern ease garments, easy access to the radio, to television, to the motion picture, newspapers and secular magazines, worldly amusements of all kinds, easy chairs and couches, cooling devices, unrestricted use of the automobile. —A community can employ *safeguards*. And each one must decide what *permitted* comforts are permissible *for him*.

When a dollar or so is sent by a relative for a treat, the giver usually says: "Get yourself something." Must that money thus given to a religious definitely be set aside for the treat?

Catholic relatives know to some extent at least that their religious relative or friend is bound by the vow of poverty and by other regulations. Hence, when they make a gift with the words: "Get yourself something," they merely express a wish or a hope that the religious will be able to use it for that purpose. They give the gift from a motive of liberality, as a rule. They do not want to embarrass the recipient, so they ordinarily want her to do as she has to do with the gift. In this case the Sister simply has to hand it over to the superior for the common treasury, from which all the religious are supplied with what is needed. Though a Sister could say it was given that she might get herself something, and though the superior could then give her permission to get herself what she wants, it would be more virtuous simply to put her gift at the disposition of the community.

If a relative should give a gift with words like these: "Here you have five dollars, but I am giving it to you only on condition that you get yourself this or that, otherwise I won't give it to you," and then the Sister accepts it, she must use it for that purpose and no

other. It must be used for the purpose specified, or
refused. A religious should have the courage to refuse
such a gift.

If a religious receives a donation for transmission
to a certain missionary priest, for instance, she does
not offend against poverty by accepting it and sending
it on, unless she asked for it contrary to a rule that
says one may not ask for anything for oneself or for
others without permission. However, she might sin
against obedience if there is a rule which forbids her
thus to transmit donations.

This leads us to the consideration of Mass stipends.
Mass stipends are an offering, a donation, given with
the express intention that a Mass be offered according to the donor's specified intention, or a number of
Masses, as the case may be. If a Sister would in any
way receive a Mass stipend to be given by her to some
priest and if she accepts it, she has a serious obligation to transmit it, to see to it that the Mass is offered.
Hence, if someone would say: "Here are three dollars,
for one purpose only: to have three Masses offered for
yourself, as a gift from me," and the Sister would
gratefully accept the donation, she would have a serious obligation to have three Masses offered for herself—a blessed obligation. She may simply give it to a
priest to have the Masses said, or have the superior do
so if she wishes. A donation is merely being trans-
mitted, from the donor to the priest. It is accidental
that the Masses are to be offered for the Sister. She
receives a spiritual benefit not valuable in money.
There is here no violation of poverty. If the rule forbids her to accept such Mass stipends, and she does so
without permission, she sins against obedience, but
not against poverty. And it is hard for us to imagine a
rule that would forbid this.

VI

CHASTITY

I would like to have some instruction on the vow of chastity. To what are we bound when we make this vow?

Chastity is a virtue which restrains the inordinate desire of indulgence in sexual pleasures and excludes sinful thoughts, words, and deeds contrary to purity. There is the chastity of virgins, or widows and widowers, and of the married. Virginal chastity, with which we are concerned in this reply, is a firm and effective resolve of the will to abstain from every willful venereal act, whether internal or external.

When sealed by a solemn promise, by the vow of chastity, in an order approved by the Church, it constitutes religious chastity. This vow imposes upon the religious two obligations: 1. to forego marriage; 2. to avoid every exterior or interior act already forbidden by the sixth and the ninth commandments of God. This vow adds a new obligation to that of those two commandments; and if a religious violates his vow he commits a second sin, the sin of sacrilege, which he must also tell in confession unless the confessor already knows that he is bound by vow. Moreover, if the sin is exterior, it often means a third sin, the deplorable sin of scandal that brands the whole religious institute or community with the infamy attached to this sort of a sin.

Hence, every religious must be chaste in mind and body. Every infraction of the virtue of chastity is also a violation of the vow: there is no distinction here. All sins directly against chastity, if committed *with full deliberation* and *full consent,* are mortal; hence, even interior complacency and unchaste desires, if *fully deliberate* and *voluntary.* Unchaste words spoken out of levity (though this is really unthinkable in a religious), looks upon persons of the other sex out of curiosity, are not in themselves mortal sins. They are committed without any complacency, as we suppose. Then, too, not every bad thought is blameworthy, but only those which come from our own will, which we recall or entertain freely through affection for evil, for which we are responsible. Those which come from the enemy of our salvation or from an evil inclination which is in us in spite of ourselves do not belong to us and we are not responsible for them, as long as we do not want them, do not consent to them, try to exclude them. Indeed, far from offending God, we then, by resisting a bad thought, have the merit of overcoming a temptation. We can thus show our love for God in deed. "My God, I love Thee more than *that*." The greater the temptation, the greater the merit when we overcome it.

The same may be said of bad impressions that may be felt in the senses. We are not responsible for those which we do not directly cause, in which the will does not take a free part, which we disclaim with all our heart. They leave us blameless and even give us a chance of practicing real virtue. In the midst of all such temptations or natural feelings we must keep in mind that, when we took the vow of chastity, we gave God a great gift, and that to sacrifice sexual desires and give them back to God we must first have the sincerity and humility to recognize that they are there to be offered to God by sacrifice in the religious state.

Will you please give me some motives for the practice of chastity?

The essence of chastity is the religious respect which man owes to himself. Motives for this respect are: 1. that man is divinely loved by God, 2. that man is the property of God. Hence chastity is fidelity. You are His spouse. "I will espouse thee to Me in faith; and thou shalt know that I am the Lord" (Osee 2:20).

The study of the divine perfections is an aid to chastity. Be convinced that God is perfect Beauty, supreme Goodness, infinite Love, absolute Joy, and chastity will never fail nor perish. When temptation comes, meditate on that and say from the heart: "I love Thee more than this, O Beauty from which all beauty comes."

Recently the Sacred Congregation in Charge of the Affairs of Religious granted an indult for the reception of the Consecration of Virgins. It was extended to certain Sisters in North America. Does one's eligibility to making this complete consecration demand the inviolability of virginity?

This question is sufficiently answered by the following extracts from the document of the promulgation of the indult by the Most Reverend Bernard Kaelin, O.S.B., Abbot Primate, concerning the privilege of the Consecration of Virgins granted to the Benedictine Sisters of North America, October 24, 1950:

"Regarding the inviolability of virginity as an essential qualification, we may say that all who have never been married may be admitted to the ceremony, provided they have vowed themselves to God in perpetuity. The forum of conscience is not to be infringed upon. [The forum of conscience is not to be infringed upon—repeated by us for emphasis.] One who has dedicated herself to God in the state of virginity in contradistinction to the state of matrimony is eligible for the privilege."

"In the early Church, the age for this complete consecration to God was forty years. This need not be adhered to in the use of the privilege. It might be wise to defer the consecration until some years after perpetual vows as an incentive for a deeper and more mature spirituality. Some think that ten years after perpetual vows would be a mature time."

Here it may be well to recall the comforting assurance given by St. Augustine, who had sad experiences of his own before his conversion: *Longa castitas reputatur pro virginitate:* a long practice of chastity counts for virginity.

What is the most effective means to combat and overcome temptations?

We are told that four hermits once discussed this problem. The first one said that the best means to overcome the temptations of the devil was to think of hell. Something like this, I suppose: If there were an eternity reserved for me in hell, what a terrible misery! Always the stain of sin; always the outer darkness; always the gnawing of worms; always the torment of fire; always imprisonment in chains; always the overflowing of tears; always the gnashing of teeth; always the blasphemies of the damned; always the torments inflicted by devils; always the overwhelming curse of God. Always? Always. And never a ray of light to give joy; never a moment of sleep to restore; never a drop of water to refresh; never a friendly word to console. Never to see God, never!

The second said that the most effective means was to reflect upon the vileness of the devil, who tempted Adam and Eve and even dared to tempt the Savior Himself. Some time ago a book entitled *Satan* was published. It is about the devil. The volume we received had a double jacket, with the explanation that the original jacket drawn by an artist who sought to make Satan as horribly repulsive as possible, aroused such revulsion and loathing in the minds of those who saw it that there was a pressing demand that it be removed. That was in France. The publishers so far acceded to this demand as to put two jackets on the book. We kept the hideous thing that was supposed to represent Satan. But the oftener we looked at it, the more horror and disgust it seemed to generate within us. Finally we tore it to shreds.

The third hermit said that the most effective means to combat temptations is the consideration of the vileness, loathsomeness, and ingratitude of sin. If even a picture of the devil fills one with horror, dread, and detestation, what ought not the contemplation of sin do. A simple way of meditating on sin in order to detest it and be sorry for it and avoid it is to make St. Charles Borromeo's four stations, as they are called. First go to an open grave and look down upon the rotting, worm-eaten corpse (and think of all who have ever died and will die)—sin brought death into the world. Then look down into hell, the second station, and see the awful sufferings of the demons and the damned in that place of everlasting fire—sin made hell. At the third station look up into heaven, see the beauty and bliss of the saved, of that multitude of blessed ones—by sin one can lose that eternity of inconceivable blessing, the supreme happiness that always lasts and never will end. Think: always truth and virtue, life and bliss, the blessed and the angels, always God to contemplate, to love, to possess, to bless; and never more any tears, or death, or sorrow, or mourning, never. Finally, at the fourth station, look upon Christ dying on the cross and consider that by sin we crucify unto ourselves the Son of God anew and make a mockery of Him.

This leads us to what the fourth hermit looked upon as the most effective means to overcome the temptations of the devil. He said it was the consideration of our Lord's bitter passion and death. If anyone is not inflamed with the love of God by contemplating Jesus dead upon the cross, he will never love at all. We are to reflect upon the words: "God so loved the world as to give His only-begotten Son." Love demands love in return; and we love God by keeping

His commandments, which the tempter urges us to break: "He that has My commandments and keeps them, he is the one who loves Me."

Imagine the Savior in agony on the cross for three hours, without any relief. If He rested His head, He found the thorns piercing still deeper; if He threw Himself forward, the wounds opened still wider; wherever He turned His eyes, He met something tormenting: here His Mother in desolation; there, a robber who outraged Him; all around the Jews, who insulted Him; and eclipse in the heavens, darkness in the air, earthquakes on the earth. Amidst so many sorrows He had no one to give Him assistance. He asked for some relief to assuage His thirst, and he was given gall and vinegar. He could not get help from His disciples, for they had all fled and deserted Him; nor from His Mother, because it was not permitted by the executioners. Besides, she was so feeble and exhausted that she required someone to console herself. Even the eternal Father appears to have abandoned Him, so that the afflicted Savior cried out in the depth of His desolation: "My God, My God, why hast Thou forsaken Me?" Thus martyred by interior grief, bloody and bruised and wounded in all His members, His death agony began. His countenance grew pale, His lips became livid, His chest swelled, His eyes closed, He bowed His head and breathed His last sigh. Draw a mental picture of it all when in temptation and see written beneath that picture: "Nobody Cares!"—and care.

I have been told so often to pray in temptation, to start at once, resisting the beginnings, and persevere in prayer. Sometimes in temptation I say a whole rosary for the poor souls, or a litany for poor sinners,

*and it all does not seem to help much. What do you
think is wrong?*

In temptation you should pray particularly for one
thing: to be delivered from the evil that threatens
you. It should be, not just prayer, any prayer, but
prayer against the evil itself. "O God deliver me from
this, help me overcome this, make me strong against
this. Jesus, Mary, help! Jesus, Mary!" And repeat
fervently those holy and powerful names, ten times,
twenty times, a hundred times, until you have overcome the temptation. You always will. If you say the
rosary or litany or some other prayers, say them especially in order to be delivered from the temptation.

Often after a temptation you will wonder whether
God still loves you, whether you are still in the grace
of God. You will wish that you knew for certain. Then
take to heart these words of St. Alphonsus: "You desire to know for certain that God loves you? But at
the moment He does not will to impart to you this
knowledge. He wills that you should just humble
yourself, trust in His goodness, and resign yourself
wholly to His good pleasure. Besides, it is a maxim,
received as incontestable by all the masters of the
spiritual life, that when a person of timorous conscience is in doubt as to whether he has lost the grace
of God, it is certain that he has not lost it. For no one
can lose God without being fully aware of the fact.
Moreover, according to St. Francis de Sales, the resolution you have, at least in the depths of your heart, to
love God and not to cause Him the slightest displeasure by deliberate purpose, is a manifest sign that you
are still in His grace. Abandon yourself, therefore,
into the arms of divine mercy, protest that you desire
nothing but God alone and His good pleasure, and

banish every fear. Oh, how agreeable to the Lord are the acts of confidence and resignation we make in the midst of this terrifying darkness."

And Lehodey says: "Let souls of good will take courage. In the senses and the imagination many things can happen which are not voluntary acts, and consequently not sins. We have really resisted as we should, but the enveloping darkness prevents us from seeing distinctly what has taken place. The will, however, has undergone no change. Experience will soon show that. Let us meet an occasion of offending God by a simple deliberate venial sin, and we shall scrupulously abstain from it: we should prefer to die a thousand times. It ought to be enough for us to know that we have watched and prayed, generously struggled. There is no necessity that we should have a clear consciousness of victory won. It is sometimes better for us to be without such knowledge, as the incertitude can be very profitable to our humility. God wills to make us realize by painful experiences, frequently repeated, the fund of corruption we bear within ourselves, and which, without assistance of His grace, would lead us infallibly into the worst disorders. The evidence of victory would diminish the humiliation, might even expose our humility to danger. He therefore leaves us in doubt, in order to deepen the humiliation and so safeguard our humility. It is a bitter trial, but it renders us the magnificent service of solidly establishing our souls in a virtue which is the groundwork of perfection. Under such circumstances, we may even feel doubtful as to the state of our souls. Have we succumbed to the force of temptation? Are we still in the grace of God? We must not be overanxious to reassure ourselves on this point."

Here we may perhaps apply also these words of

St. Margaret Mary Alacoque in one of her letters:
"Abandon yourself blindly, full of faith and confidence, to the care of His loving providence. Never
turn back. For by taking too much care of yourself
you will prevent Him from taking care of you as He
wishes. Without your being aware of it, He will cause
you to make more progress in a month than you
would ever be able to make in the ordinary way.
What have you to fear in a way as safe as that of
humiliations? The best humiliations are those we do
not recognize as such. For humility has this pecu-
liarity: it disappears as soon as one notices it in oneself."

*Sometimes everything goes along so nicely and
smoothly and peacefully in my spiritual life for a
longer time, and I feel that I am quite ready to die
and go home to Jesus—and then all of a sudden temptations come again and I become disturbed and not so
sure that I am ready to die after all and afraid that I
have offended God. What should I do when this fear
of having offended God comes over me?*

De Caussade says: "For one who loves God, there
can be nothing more afflicting than the fear of offending Him, nothing more horrible than to have the
mind filled with evil thoughts and to feel the heart
drawn away by the force of temptation, despite one's
best efforts. But have you never meditated on the
numerous passages of Holy Scripture where the Spirit
of God teaches us the necessity of temptations and the
precious advantages they procure for souls that do not
allow themselves to be overcome? Do you not know
that temptations are compared to the furnace where
clay acquires its firmness and gold its splendor? that
they are represented as a subject for joy, as a sign

of God's friendship, as lessons indispensable for the acquisition of the science of the saints? If you bore these consoling truths in mind, how could you allow yourself to fall into the gulf of sadness? True, such temptations never come from God, but is it not He who always permits them for our good? And ought we not to adore these holy permissions in everything, outside of sin, which He detests and which we should also detest? Be careful, then, not to let yourself be troubled or disquieted by temptations. That would be worse than the temptations themselves."

Of course, you should distrust yourself, take precautions to avoid temptations, as far as in you lies, and shun occasions of sin; but excessive fear would be an illusion. If we have recourse to God, we may always be sure of victory. St. Alphonsus says: "He who has recourse to God in temptations triumphs; he who has not, suffers defeat: particularly in temptations to incontinence."

Even the holiest persons had to support these painful combats. To confine ourselves to temptations against the angelic virtue, some of the saints were entirely exempt from these, for instance, St. Teresa the Elder, St. Rose of Lima, St. Therese of the Child Jesus. Others suffered the humiliation of them only in a passing way: St. Magdalen de Pazzi during nine days, St. Margaret Mary for a few hours. Several, after one decisive victory, were thenceforward preserved altogether from them, as St. Bernard, St. Benedict, and St. Thomas Aquinas. But a very large number had to bear with the bitterness of this most afflicting trial during long years, or even to the end of their lives. The Apostle of the Gentiles, St. Frances of Rome, St. Catherine of Siena, St. Benedict Labre, and so many others were cruelly buffeted by this angel of

Satan. In the case of St. Alphonsus Rodriguez, the temptation lasted seven years; St. Mary of Egypt suffered from it seventeen years; and the Venerable Caesar de Bus twenty-five years. It attacked with terrible violence, and during the space of more than twelve months, the illustrious St. Alphonsus de Liguori, an angel of innocence, when he was in the eighty-eighth year of his age. The Blessed Angela of Foligno moves us to compassion when she tells the story of her trials.

"Blessed is the man who patiently endures trial, because after he has withstood the trial, he will receive the life-giving crown, which the Lord has promised to those that love him" (James 1:12).

I detest sin and am sedulously watchful in avoiding the occasions of sin. But at times I am terribly molested by impure and frightful thoughts and loathsome imaginations and such like things. Then I become despondent and think that God has forsaken me. What attitude of mind am I to take in this matter?

Yes, there are souls thus sorely tried. "They cannot conceive of the Holy Spirit dwelling in a soul filled with impure thoughts, and imagine themselves inevitably banished from the divine presence.

"Being thus disheartened, they are ready to despair; and half-conquered by the temptation, they think of forsaking their exercises of devotion entirely and returning to Egypt. Blind as they are, they do not see God's goodness in permitting them to be tempted as a preventive measure against human negligence, and also a coercive measure designed to bring prodigal man to closer union with his loving Father. Actually, therefore, it is most thoughtless for them to complain of that which occasions their unceasing gratitude.

"On such occasions we should consider well the perverse propensities of our wounded nature. For God, who knows best what is to our ultimate advantage, would make us aware that of ourselves we tend to nothing but sin, and when unaided by Him, fall into innumerable miseries.

"After this, we must cultivate within ourselves a loving confidence in His divine mercy, realizing that since He has been pleased to open our eyes to our danger, He also wishes to free us from it and join us to Him in prayer and confidence; for this we owe Him our most humble thanks.

"To advert again to those vile thoughts which are involuntary; it is certain that they are put to flight much sooner by a patient resignation to the anxiety they occasion, and a speedy application of the mind to something else, than by a tumultuous and over-anxious resistance" (Scupoli, *The Spiritual Combat*).

I have frequent and violent temptations against chastity and faith. I am troubled and fearful, lest I have consented. It is horrible; those temptations against chastity make an impression upon me. I actually feel an inclination toward the evil suggested. What should I do?

Do not worry. "The impression is only a sentiment. It humbles you, but it does not make you guilty. To be sensible of evil is not to consent to it. All that happens in the inferior part of the soul: imaginations, memories, feelings, irregular motions: all that is *in* us, but not *from* us. It can only become sin by our free consent. As for the inclination we feel toward evil, that is but an infirmity of our fallen nature, not a disorder of the will. Vicious pleasure solicits to evil and constitutes a danger. But it is not imputable to

us unless the will freely entertains or accepts it. However strong may be the suggestions of the demon, in
whatever form appear the phantoms that flit through
the imagination, so long as your will rejects them,
instead of soiling your soul, they rather make it
more pure and more pleasing to God. You experience
a profound and interior affliction in the temptations
to impurity, hatred, aversion, and such like. The fear
of having succumbed to them disturbs and distresses
you. That is an evident sign that you have a great fear
of God, a horror of sin, and the will to resist. Now, it
is morally impossible for a soul in such dispositions to
change suddenly so far as to give a full and entire
consent to mortal sin WITHOUT BEING
CLEARLY AWARE OF IT. At most it may happen
that, considering the force and frequency of the
temptation, there has been some little negligence, a
moment of surprise, for instance, a half-formed desire
of vengeance, semi-voluntary feelings of complacency.
But as for full, entire, and deliberate consent, that is
impossible with such a disposition of soul. Or at least
the passage from a sovereign hatred of mortal sin to a
full and free acceptance of it would be easily observed" (*Holy Abandonment,* by Lehodey, after De
Caussade).

To those golden words so worthy of careful consideration, we add these others from Grou: "Every
thought, every anxiety, which is vague, general, without any fixed and definite object, can be neither from
God nor from conscience, but exclusively from the
imagination. We are afraid of not having said all that
was necessary in confession, of having insufficiently
explained ourselves, of not having had true contrition, or lacking the right dispositions for Communion,
and so on, with a thousand other vague fears with

which we trouble and torment ourselves. Nothing of this comes from God. If He sometimes reproaches us, His reproaches have invariably some clear, precise, determinate object. We must consequently despise all such fears and courageously ignore them."

But the case would be quite different if our conscience formally accused us of something definite.

What attitude should one take as regards lustful thoughts, feelings, and desires?

In *A Retreat for Religious,* by Andrew Green, O.S.B., you will find this helpful reply: "These are all natural and gratifying to the animal man; and they will bother us even as they bothered the saints, and from time to time they will become very annoying. Any carelessness in attending to the necessities of nature, any lack of restraint in the use of intoxicants, any unguarded familiarity with the other sex, even with children, will be contributing factors to such temptations. Or it may be that we are not thoroughly humble, that we succumb to flattery and sometimes indulge in self-complacent dreaming. Now, there seems to be nothing quite so hateful to God as pride, for it robs Him of His honor; and the quickest way to bring man to his senses and to remind him that he is just nothing—and a contemptible sort of nothing— is to let him feel the sting of the flesh. God makes use of these vile temptations, not only to punish us, but also to protect us from pride or love of ease. . . . If these temptations come through no fault of ours, then we need not worry; and we will save ourselves much needless anxiety if we remember that these animal passions are a part of our make-up and are not sinful in themselves."

In temptations against purity, avoid occasions. Run away. Avoid idleness. Obey superiors cheerfully in a spirit of mortification. Never judge others rashly with regard to purity, lest God let you fall into those degrading sins.

VII

OBEDIENCE

What are the three degrees of obedience?

In St. Ignatius' *Letter on Obedience,* after speaking of the value and dignity of obedience and giving the motives for the practice of obedience (the superior takes the place of God because of God's supreme dominion over all creation; the superior takes the place of Christ because of the hierarchy He established in His Church), the Saint enumerates these three degrees of obedience:

First degree: *external* execution of the command, i.e., doing what you are told to do.

Second degree: *internal* conformity of *will* with the superior, and this as regards everything, sacrificing our will to God, and excluding all self-will.

Third degree: *internal* conformity of *mind* with the superior, which is possible because the will can command the intellect, which is necessary for the perfection of obedience and is pleasing to God, since both will and understanding are consecrated to Him.

This third degree includes so-called blind obedience, which St. Robert Bellarmine, writing on the Letter of St. Ignatius, explains by saying that "the name 'blind obedience' means nothing else than obedience which is pure, perfect, and simple, with no discussion of what is commanded or why, but remaining satisfied that a command had been given."

To acquire perfect obedience, one must be truly meek and humble of heart; and one must especially see Christ in every superior, defend in one's mind what the superior commands, and accept the superior's orders with the same unquestioning obedience which is given to God Himself, out of love for Christ. And remember that humble representation to the superior is not incompatible with perfect obedience.

How very bad is disobedience in a religious?

By disobedience you snatch back the offering which you laid upon the altar of the Most High. So it partakes of the nature of a sacrilege, the abuse of a sacred thing. One day the Savior said to St. Margaret Mary: "All religious who are not united to their superiors may look upon themselves as vessels of reprobation. . . . These souls are so far removed from My Heart that the more they try to approach Me by means of the sacraments, prayer, and other pious exercises, the further I withdraw Myself in horror from them. They will go from one hell to another, for it is this disunion that has been the loss of so many souls, and that will be the ruin of so many yet to come; because every superior, whether he is good or bad, holds My place. That is why the subject, thinking to harm the superior, inflicts so many and such mortal wounds on his own soul. After all, it is vain for him to sigh at the gates of mercy. He will not be heard, if I do not hear the voice of the superior."

But this must refer to those who are in open rebellion and contempt of their superior. For we know that one sins mortally against the vow of obedience whenever one disobeys, in a grave matter, a command of a superior given by the formulae: "In virtue of holy obedience," or "In the Name of our Lord Jesus Christ," and others of like nature, whether such a command is given in particular or in general, by spoken word or in writing, immediately or through the agency of another.

"In non-grievous matter," Cotel further says, "the superior cannot oblige under pain of mortal sin, even in virtue of the vow; but in religious communities a matter slight in itself can become serious by reason of the common interest, the end to be attained, or other circumstances."

However, from this it does not follow that the religious rarely has the merit of the vow of obedience. Why not? Because the vow always really dominates all acts of religious obedience, even when there is no actual question of its violation. The same is true of the other vows. This truth is proved by several reasons, says Cotel in *The Catechism of the Vows*:

"1. The religious, having made himself dependent in all things on the superior, is well aware in obeying that the latter can always use his right to oblige in

conscience, and thus he observes the vow by anticipat-
ing, so to speak, its obligation.

"2. Every time he submits himself to the will of the
superior, he does it in view of his vow, out of the
respect and love he has for it, and to ward off all
danger of failing in it when the superior wishes to
have recourse to the right it gives him.

"3. The observance of the vows can be compared to
that of the commandments of God. In doing, in the
same matter, more than they prescribe under pain of
sin, we observe them with more perfection and
merit."

*I find it hard always to be obedient. Can you give
me some brief principles?*

Here are some helpful principles from Archbishop
Leen: 1. The least detail of the religious rule and of
the ordinary commands of religious superiors is of
divine import. 2. The sweeping of a floor, when prescribed by the rule, is a greater act and, of course,
incomparably more meritorious than hours passed in
prayer before the Blessed Sacrament when the rule
does not permit such an employment of one's time.
3. Each little task of obligation, if acquitted in a spirit
of obedience to the divine will, has value of eternity.
"It is God's command." 4. The seclusion of Jesus during the eighteen years at Nazareth was not decided
by His own judgment that such retirement was an
apt preparation for His public career, but by the
divine will that He should submit His adolescent
judgment to His natural guardians, Mary and Joseph.

To these four principles we would add that you
should above all keep in mind that the superior takes
the place of God. This means that obedience must be
divine in intention; that is, in obeying our superiors

we must intend to obey God. We must see God in our superiors, habitually and with an often-renewed intention, not necessarily immediately always and actually, for that is hardly possible. God wills that we should thus act on faith; he gives us the grace to do so and is much pleased when we cooperate with that grace. St. Ignatius says: "Revere the divine majesty in those who command you and render them your obedience in a perfectly religious spirit."

My longing for union with Christ is so great. How can I attain to an ever closer union with Him?

As you have heard so often, self-denial for the love of Christ is the only road to perfection. "If any man will come after Me, let him take up his cross daily and follow Me." There is not enough self-denial, even among religious. Why not? Because there is not enough love of Christ.

The more you excel in the observance of your vows of poverty, chastity, and obedience, the closer you will draw to the Savior. The first foundation in the attainment of perfection, as St. Thomas tells us in the *Summa,* is voluntary poverty. "Sell what thou hast and follow Me." Union with Christ, however, comes not so much from leaving all things as from following Him. However, the desire for worldly pleasures gradually gives way to desire for union with Christ. Endeavor to cultivate a strong personal love for Christ. And then, for the love of Christ, dedicate yourself unselfishly to the love-service of others.

You yearn for union with Christ. Chastity, virginity is the consummation of love between God and the soul. It is not a frustration, but is, as in the life of our Lady, a condition of higher fruitfulness designed by God to give supernatural life to the world. You have the humility and sincerity to recognize that sexual desires are there to be offered as a sacrifice to God in the religious life, and you cheerfully offer yourself in total dedication. The foregoing of the physical expression is the means of achieving spiritual motherhood by which Sisters belong, not merely to one human family, but to all souls redeemed by the Blood of Christ. As Pope Pius XII pointed out: "Chastity and virginity . . . do not estrange souls from this world. They rather awaken and develop the energies needed for wider and higher offices beyond the limits of individual families. Today there are many teaching and nursing Sisters who, in the best sense of the word, are nearer to life than the average person in the world" (First International Congress of Religious Sisters, September 15, 1951).

The observance of the virtue and vow of obedience will lead you even more quickly and surely to union with God; for this virtue inclines you to reverence the will of God and submit yourself to it, and the vow engages you to God to obey in all that your legitimate superior enjoins. Doing the will of God is to love God, is union with God. One of the reasons why the number of those who desire to become religious is lessening is, to quote Pius XII again (December 8, 1950), "that it is found too difficult to give up personal judgment and part with freedom, all of which is implied by the vow of obedience."

You may envision a religious community as a cell in the Church, Christ's mystical body, of which Christ is the Head; and the superior is Christ's visible representative. Wherefore, though all authority comes from God, there is no authority on earth which is so exactly a sign of the authority of Christ as ecclesiastical and religious authority. Jesus Christ has all power in heaven and on earth; He has delegated this power in a solemn manner to the apostles and their successors, particularly to the Roman Pontiff. The Church in turn communicates a part of this power to the superiors general of religious orders, and these transmit it to a greater or less extent to provincials and local superiors for the immediate government of the members. Behold the series of links from the last superior up to Almighty God Himself. Hence the answer to the protest that might here be registered: "But my superior is so imperfect—God would not be like my superior," is that it is not the superior's individual qualities that represent God, but the authority delegated her by Christ. Obedience is a matter of principle, not of persons. Instead of despising the dignity because of the person, always reverence the person because of the dignity. In reality, there are not many superiors, but only one, Jesus Christ, whom we recognize in every human superior. It is Jesus Christ who changes names and countenance, but it is always Jesus Christ. He hides Himself beneath the weakness and the imperfections of man, just as He conceals Himself beneath the sacramental species. If the Pope, instead of appearing in the spotless white vesture in which we usually see him, were vested in the coarse, patched habit of some poor religious, he would nevertheless be the visible representative of Christ on earth.

Christ was subject to His Father from the beginning: "In the head of the book it is written of me that I should do thy will." All His life long it was His meat to do the will of His Father. He was subject to Joseph and Mary. To Pilate He said: "Thou wouldst not have any power over me, if it were not given thee from above." And He was obedient unto death, even unto the death of the cross. For us religious, then, it is an article of faith that our superiors are God's representatives and rule by His authority and power.

I am unhappy in my community because of the position I occupy—just stuck into a corner doing nothing of any account. What should I do?

Do the will of God with a glad and happy heart. It is now His will that you be stuck in that corner doing nothing of any account, as you say. If you are dissatisfied, thinking that you and your talents are fitted for something better than you are doing, reflect that you were born to love and serve God and to live with Him forever hereafter. Think of the Divine Savior, who spent about ten times as many years hidden away in that corner called Nazareth as in the public eye. And why? Because it was the Father's will. "I have given you an example." When you are in those despondent moods, it would be well to study our Lord's life at Nazareth, that sleepy little village of which it has been said: "Can any good thing come out of Nazareth?"— "In that little village home, with a simple village maid for His Mother, He spent thirty years of His life. Of course, He might have chosen a very different kind of life, but He selected this kind of life to be a lesson to us. We are too much inclined to look down upon our less fortunate neighbors, and to be jealous of those above us, but, after all, these things are of no account before God, and social distinctions make no difference before Him."

The Savior chose Mary instead of some grand queen; He chose to come as a babe instead of as a full grown man; He chose to come to a poor house in Nazareth instead of to a Caesar's palace; He chose to lead a hidden life, doing nothing special, but fulfilling the will of God.

The will of God alone matters. He has known everything about you from all eternity. Where you are now, and what you are doing or not doing, is His will, all in His divine plan. Be happy!

Speaking of obedience in the Constitutions of the Society of Jesus, St. Ignatius says: "Suppressing all contrary opinion and judgment of our own with a sort of blind obedience." In what way is such perfect obedience blind?

Such obedience is blind because it does not see the defects of the person of the superior whom God has placed over us, though the eyes and ears of the body cannot but perceive them.

It is blind because once we see the ordinance of the superior as the will of God in our regard, we simply do not look any farther; we don't look, don't seem to see the nature of the command as regards our likes or dislikes.

Such obedience is blind inasmuch as we simply obey, seeming not to see the reasons opposing the decision of the superior—at least after we have respectfully and submissively made them known to him, as we always may do and sometimes must do. Above our own reasons is the one reason which makes all other contrary reasons invalid and, as it were, non-existent for us—the transcendent will of God.

We should daily pray: "Divine Savior, grant us the virtue of religious obedience, Thou who for us didst become obedient unto death, even the death of the cross, in order that we may not do our will but may at all times do the will of our superiors, in which we see and venerate Thine own."

Blind obedience makes the superior's policies the policies of the community, of all the members of the community; it changes all the policies of every member of the community when the superior changes his policies, or when the superior is changed, or when a new superior with new policies enters into authority.

Religious often hear and read of blind and corpse-like obedience. (A corpse has no will of its own: put it in a certain place and it stays there.) That means, to repeat, that one must obey *as though* one were blind and dead. It does not mean that in obeying one must neither see nor be alive. That would make religious men and women into automata. It would make them into docile idiots and inert dummies, and that would be contrary to common sense and to the common good.

Suppose you have perfectly plain reasons for thinking that your lawful superior is making a mistake, that he is not well informed about matters and so lacks the requisite knowledge to command aright, or that he is swayed by some passion, or that he gives the command under the urge of ambition, or selfish designs, or spite, or getting even. Suppose all this and more. Provided he has the right to order what he actually does order, it is your plain duty to obey perfectly in carrying out his command, the imperfection of which you recognize in the speculative order but which you nevertheless accept, judging the command to be wise for you on account of the authority that imposes it. Your superior may indeed be wrong; but you cannot be wrong in obeying him in all that is not sin.

VIII

CHARITY

What can I do to overcome my uncharitableness?

Make a meditation on the Savior washing the feet of His disciples. Remember that they wore sandals and had come through unsanitary streets and that, accordingly, their feet were dirty, filthy, repulsive. And the immortal Son of God kneels down and washes them! Imitate Him! Imagine the Savior washing the feet of Peter, His friend. He washed his feet *because* he was His friend. Even if you cannot help seeing the faults of others, disregard them, give them a charitable interpretation, bear with them because you know that,

even if it is not God's signified will that your neighbor has those faults, it is the will of His good pleasure
that you bear with them, considering your own innumerable sins, offenses, and negligences. Most of those
who surround us are our friends. In an ordinary community we could all say with truth: "Everybody here
loves me with a real Christian charity." That is but
keeping the great commandment: "A new commandment I give to you, that you love one another as I have
loved you."

Jesus washed the feet of Judas *because* he was His
enemy. Those feet would soon be hastening away to
betray the Master; they would lead that band of men
into the Garden of Olives to seize Him and lead Him
away to His Passion and death. Even if your fellow
religious should, by way of exception, be your enemy,
you must have charity toward the same. The Savior
said: "You have heard that it was said, 'Thou shalt
love thy neighbor, and shalt hate thy enemy.' But I
say to you, love your enemies, do good to those who
persecute and calumniate you, so that you may be
children of your Father in heaven, who makes his sun
to rise on the good and the evil, and sends rain on the
just and the unjust. . . . You are therefore to be perfect, even as your heavenly Father is perfect" (Matt.
5:43, 45, 48).

How can you be uncharitable when you have before
you the Savior on His knees, girded with a towel,
washing the feet of His disciples?

*In the matter of Christian charity, how should a
Sister re-act when apologies are refused? Try as I will,
Sister X will have no part of me. This bothers me
greatly, even though my confessor assures me that
since I have sincerely tried to make up, my obligation*

is over with. This has been going on for some months, and it seems so uncalled for, and anything but religious-like. Retreat time will soon be here and I sure would like this "healed" before then.

Poor Sister X! She should read and meditate on the pertinent truths of divine revelation. "By this shall all men know that you are my disciples, if you have love one for another" (John 13:35). "Thou shalt love the Lord thy God with thy whole heart and with thy whole soul and with thy whole mind and with thy whole strength. This is the first commandment. And the second is like to it: Thou shalt love thy neighbor as thyself. There is no other commandment greater than these. And the scribe said to Him: Well, Master, Thou hast said in truth that . . . to love one's neighbor as one's self is a greater thing than all holocausts and sacrifices. And Jesus seeing that he had answered wisely said to him: Thou art not far from the kingdom of God" (Mark 12:28 ff.). "God is charity: and he that abideth in charity abideth in God, and God in him" (1 John 4:16). "My dearest, if God hath so loved us, we also ought to love one another. . . . If we love one another, God abideth in us: and His charity is perfected in us" (1 John 4:11, 12). "We know that we have passed from death to life, because we love the brethren" (1 John 3:14). "But before all things have a constant mutual charity among yourselves: for charity covereth a multitude of sins" (1 Peter 4:8). "If you will forgive men their offenses, your heavenly Father will forgive you also your offenses. But if you will not forgive men, neither will your Father forgive you your offenses" (Matt. 6:14, 15). "A new commandment I give unto you: That you love one another, as I have loved you" (John 13:34). "This is my com-

mandment, that you love one another, as I have loved
you" (John 15:12). "He that loveth not, abideth in
death . . . he that loveth not, knoweth not God: for
God is charity" (1 John 3:14; 4:8). "If therefore thou
offer thy gift at the altar, and there thou remember
that thy brother hath anything against thee: leave
there thy offering before the altar and go first to be
reconciled to thy brother: and then coming thou shalt
offer thy gift" (Matt. 5:23, 24).

Some principles: 1. Act at once and do not coddle
and nurse the rankling wound when you feel the sting
of injury. Remember that the Savior is unbending,
unmoving, and unrelenting on this point. Forgive if
you wish to be forgiven. He told Peter that he must
forgive the offending brother, not till seven times, but
till seventy times seven times (see Matt. 18); this
means that there is no limit at which unforgiveness
may set in. 2. No matter what gifts of prayer, Communions, Masses, sacrifices you may bring, God refuses every gift from a Sister who refuses Him the one
great gift He desires most of her: genuine charity and
whole-souled forgiveness of those who have injured
her, together with the rightful adjustment of and a
fair indemnity for the injuries she inflicted on others.
3. Only in very unusual cases is a formal and cere-
monious apology called for in the matter of effecting
a reconciliation. The Sisters concerned should simply
act toward one another as if nothing had happened
to cause any wilful ill feeling, or at least pass it up
and attach no further importance to it, or at any rate
not let it interfere with their observance of the great
commandment of love of the neighbor. 4. If there is
question only of a fancied grievance which another
has against us, which is not due to any fault of ours
but to a queer mental quirk or emotional disorder,

we have no obligation to make apologies which no one has a right to expect of us. But in this matter we must beware of self-delusion. Rather abound than run the risk of lacking in the spirit of forgiveness. 5. It is not against the spirit of forgiveness prudently and charitably to avoid creating situations in which others may be tempted to repeat their injury and abuse. Hence it is not wrong to observe a prudent reserve toward and a kindly aloofness from such as do not get on well with us at close range and in familiar converse.

It is in this last directive that you will find how you should react when apologies are refused.

And, as regards the hard and unrelenting Sister, let her keep in mind these words of our Lord: "Thou wicked servant, I forgave thee all the debt, because thou besoughtest Me: shouldst not thou then have compassion also on thy fellow servant, even as I had compassion on thee?" (Matt. 18:32)

Under what conditions would one be allowed to say something uncomplimentary about another individual without wounding charity?

Under no circumstances, let us say, unless it be a matter of duty, as when we have to report certain things according to the rules, or when we are in an official position and have to discuss the characters of persons with a view to elections, appointments, and the like; but even then one should be as restrained and charitable as possible.

In order to avoid idle talkativeness and thoughtless gossip that does injury to one's neighbor and thus wounds charity, the following points will be helpful.

1. To say of a person that he is ignorant, dull, imprudent, or to say that he is proud, avaricious, hot-

tempered, lazy, is ordinarily not a mortal sin, because those things are natural defects and faults that are not serious.

2. To speak generalities about the faults of others is not a mortal sin; but it may be if you say, for example, that you know something about such and such a person which charity forbids you to reveal.

3. To tell things about a person as heard by you from others may, according to circumstances, be a mortal sin against justice or charity. It would be a venial sin or no sin if you foresee that those who are listening to you will not believe you.

4. There is no detraction when you mention faults already publicly known or if they are commonly known or soon will be generally known. But a fact formerly a matter of public knowledge and now forgotten may not be brought to light again if the guilty person has mended his ways.

5. To talk about the evident vices of a people or of a whole nation in general is not sinful, because you are speaking about something well known or about a national characteristic; you are speaking about many in general and not about personal sins.

6. Chaff or banter or teasing, which is not intended to wound or irritate others, is, of course, no sin, so long as it keeps within proper bounds.

7. Mockery or derision makes sport of another's honor. You can be very uncharitable in this way by employing the faults and infirmities of others to make them the butt of laughter or contempt.

8. As regards the particular respect and reverence which you, as a citizen of your country, owe to the higher administrative officials to whom the execution of the laws is entrusted, you might remember that criticism or gossip about real and known defects is

sinful if there is no sufficient reason for it. The sin committed is usually that of idle talk or uncharitableness. One disedifies the listeners, causes sadness to the person gossiped about, gives vent to one's spitefulness. Criticism thus understood is dangerous because it prepares the way for detraction and calumny. It is to be noted here that the law does indeed permit fair comment on public persons or works, but it likewise grants an action for criticism that contains unfair aspersions of personal character or unjust accusations about personal conduct. People often go to shocking extremes in this matter in our country.

IX

SPIRITUAL EXERCISES

Doesn't the particular examen, in which one counts up one's faults, lead one to be overanxious about the faults and get into what has been called "an everlasting scraping away at oneself"?

St. Ignatius Loyola does not think so. In *The Spiritual Exercises* he says that the particular examen is to be made daily and that it includes three times of the day and two examinations. We quote the directions:

"The first time is the morning: straightway on rising the person must resolve to guard himself with diligence against that particular sin or defect which he desires to correct and amend.

"The second time is after the midday meal, when he is to ask of God our Lord that which he wants, that is to say, grace to remember how often he has fallen into that particular sin or defect, and to amend in future; and accordingly let him make the first examination demanding an account from his soul concerning the particular thing proposed, which he desires to correct and amend, reviewing the time that has elapsed, hour by hour, or period by period, from the hour of rising till the hour and moment of the present examination, and let him mark on the first line of the diagram as many points as there are times he has fallen into that particular sin or defect; and then let him resolve anew to amend himself until the second examination that he will make.

"The third time is after supper, when the second examination will be made in like manner, hour by hour, beginning from the first examination to this second one. Let him mark on the second line of the same diagram as many points as there are times he has fallen into that particular sin or defect."

Such is the particular examen as taught by St. Ignatius. It may be summed up in *resolving, praying, watching, examining, comparing* (one week with another). Different communities have different times for the examen; but essentially it is the same.

St. Ignatius taught the negative particular examen, for the rooting out of defects and sins. He does not, however, require that the defect which we want to correct should always be our besetting defect, our predominant fault, our "pet sin."

Still, one may also practice the positive particular examen endeavoring to implant in ourselves a particular virtue and thus avoid defects contrary to it. Some think this method is psychologically more correct, inasmuch as the best way of resisting the attacks of our enemy on the weakest part of the fortress of our soul is by strengthening it. They think, as implied in your question, that to fight directly against a defect may end in implanting it more vividly in our sensitive faculties.

So it really doesn't matter much whether we carefully avoid a defect and thereby implant the opposite virtue, or give ourselves to a particular virtue and thus avoid defects contrary to it. In the first case we have the negative particular examen; in the second, the positive. Some like the positive examen better, especially those who do not like the idea of "an everlasting scraping away at oneself."

What is the difference between mental and vocal prayer?

Prayer is the lifting up of the mind and heart to God to adore Him, to thank Him for the benefits we have received from Him, to beg His forgiveness, to ask Him for all the graces we need, whether for soul or body. Prayer is an act of the virtue of religion and may be vocal (interior prayer expressed in words) or mental (interior prayer without words). Real prayer, then, is always to some extent interior.

Now we can better understand what St. Theresa means when she says in effect that, when the terms *vocal* and *mental* prayer are properly understood, they are one and the same thing. When vocal prayer is properly said, with understanding of what we are doing and with complete sincerity (and these are best attained in solitude), it becomes mental prayer. This ought to be a source of consolation for so many reli-

gious who have to intersperse so many vocal prayers
in their mental prayer that they wonder whether or
not they are making a meditation. Mental prayer is
"to think and to understand what we are saying, and
with Whom we speak, and who we are who dare to
talk to so great a Lord. To think this and other similar
things, of how little we have served Him and how
much we ought to serve Him, is mental prayer"
(*Escorial*, p. 292). We ourselves, by our own will and
determination, can make all our vocal prayer into
mental prayer, according to the above; this may not
meet the approval of some, but will be a consolation
to many more. Contemplation is, of course, a different
matter, though it is not so unusual at all for a fervent,
observant religious to practice that common contemplation which is simply an awareness of the being and
presence of God.

*How about this case? Regular confessors are as-
signed as ordinary confessors for the weekly confessions of all the Sisters. In that same chapel the chaplain also hears confessions daily for those who wish
to go. May a Sister, for convenience' sake or because she receives more spiritual direction from him
than from the ordinary confessors, go to confession
regularly to the chaplain, as if he were one of the
ordinary confessors?*

For peace of conscience a Sister may go at any time
to receive the sacrament of penance from any duly
approved priest. Every Sister knows that. However,
that is not the situation which is envisioned here.
From the wording of the question above, it seems
evident that the chaplain, in addition to the regular
faculties, has also the faculty to hear the confessions of
religious women. Such a priest may then validly and

licitly hear the confessions of the Sisters. Nor does he require the permission of the Superioress or the explicit consent of the Ordinary, that is, of the bishop. He has been given those special faculties by the bishop, presumably just because he is in a situation in which he will be called upon to use them, as in the case presented here. Without being designated as one of the ordinary confessors, he seems to be an undesignated one.

Sisters should not always be going to some other priest for peace of conscience, making him as it were their ordinary confessor. That would not be acting according to the mind of the Church, which requires that ordinary and extraordinary confessors be appointed, for the sake of uniformity in spiritual direction, or to give the Sisters a definite choice, when they prefer the guidance of one confessor to that of another. However, it is only to the extraordinary confessor that they are *obliged* to present themselves four times a year, at least to receive his blessing.

Canon 520 ordains that only one ordinary confessor should be designated for each convent, that this confessor should hear the confessions of all the Sisters. But in the case of a very large number of Sisters, or for other weighty reasons, it may be necessary to designate two or more ordinary confessors.

As we have said above, it is the wish of the Church that the spiritual direction of each convent be in the hands of one priest, so that there may be unity in all that is undertaken for the good of the Sisters. But, as we have also said, often two or more are appointed for weighty reasons. In the case here presented, two or more do hear the confessions regularly. And in addition to those two or more, there is also the chaplain, who daily hears the confessions of those Sisters who may wish to go. The supposition is, of course, that he has special faculties to hear the confessions of Sisters, just as the ordinary and extraordinary confessors have. He is, to all intents and purposes, in the same category as an ordinary confessor. It would seem, then, that just as a certain Sister may go now to one, then to another, of the designated confessors, or may go always to one and the same, so she may likewise always go to the chaplain if she so desires. That she may do so is no doubt the very reason why he has such special faculties. He is, in effect at least, a supplementary confessor.

Some religious day after day receive Holy Communion with apparently commendable recollection and piety, and yet they seem to manifest a disheartening lack of spirituality in their daily life in general. How is that to be explained?

Sad to say, there are such religious. They lack a real spirit of mortification, not even taking the trouble to observe the rules they promised to live by; they are averse to the least self-sacrifice. They easily yield to resentment and hurt feelings, being sensitive and touchy to a degree. They are envious and jealous, and it is so hard to avoid slighting them or offending them in some way by lack of attention. Wrong them in the least, and they will nurse a grudge and keep telling themselves that they are justified in their antipathies. They are frequently irritable, impatient, and disobliging, and often sour and self-centered and morose. When their arrangements are interfered with and they are obliged to vary the order of existence they have planned for themselves, they give proof of their ill humor.

The trouble seems to be, as regards the little effect that Communion has upon them, that they approach the Holy Table with a heart divided between themselves and the Lord. Self gets the lion's share. They surrender themselves but partially, and accept Jesus but partially. They do not dispose themselves as they ought for the reception of Holy Communion. Real devotedness is wanting.

Is it true that the retreat masters religious get for their annual retreats are not always the best in every way?

We asked some veteran Sisters about this. One said: "I was always happy and satisfied about all my retreat masters. They were all good. I liked them all. May our good Lord bless and reward them!" Another replied: "I have made a retreat in the convent every year for over thirty years and I must honestly say that I enjoyed each and every one of them, always getting out of them something that was just fitting for me. And every year I eagerly look forward to that happy time." Another answered: "I can sincerely say that I always was satisfied with my retreat master, no matter who it was. After all, it's always up to me to carry on the retreat after it is over. No one can make me holy if I do not work along with the grace of God."

We might be inclined to say that those Sisters were simple souls. They say that it does not matter who the retreat master is. It is the retreatant who makes the retreat. The retreat master merely directs. It is up to the retreatant. All of this is true enough. And yet it does make a difference who he is and how he gives the retreat.

Yet that difference should not be so great as to lead one to say that such and such a retreat master was a complete failure. Let every religious be cautious in making such a statement. Others in that same retreat

may have found him quite satisfactory, remember, or
could sincerely say that he was the best ever, or even
found before the retreat was over that he was a man
sent by God for their sanctification and salvation.
Even if we are somewhat or completely disappointed,
let us be slow in indulging the supposition that others
feel the way we do about the retreat master. Personally, we have made many retreats with many different
retreat masters, members of different religious orders,
and we can sincerely say that we have found every one
of them a real man of God, at whose piety, zeal, knowledge, we marveled, from whose considerations we
derived great benefit. Some indeed spoke too fast, so
that we could not understand much of what was said;
others did not speak loud enough for the place they
were in, so that it took an effort to follow the dis-
course; others spoke too loud, shouted so much that
one charitably wondered why all that effort was use-
lessly expended; some never told a single story or used
a single concrete illustration to sustain interest and
drive home a point, whereas others told one story after
the other, to the delight of these and the chagrin of
those; some never so much as smiled during the whole
retreat, while others had a superabundance of the
saving sense of humor and kept you trying to suppress
your laughter. Again, some followed the Ignatian
method; others, some other official method; and many
followed a method which was all their own. But they
were all good, each in his own way. God bless them all.
Some day, in heaven, we shall meet again. How interesting it will be to examine into the keeping of those
good resolutions.

So it is true enough that the retreat masters religious get for their annual retreats are not always the
best in every way—those men themselves would be the

last ones to claim that—but they are all good. And
sometimes you will get one who is better. And occasionally you will get the best ever!

We spoke about the saving sense. There was the
retreat master who gave a retreat to a community of
Sisters one year. Before another year passed, he was
elected superior of his house, unbeknown to the
Sisters mentioned. Lo and behold! in the course of
time he got a letter from the Mother Superior to this
effect: "Dear Father Superior, please send us a retreat
master for our annual retreat this year. But for
heaven's sake do not send the one we had last year!"
Last year's retreat master, superior now, got a good
laugh out of it. Life is like that.

*What is the best manner of making the way of the
cross? I mean when a religious makes it privately.*

There are different ways of making the stations
privately, for instance, with a book or without a book,
making a genuflection at each station or kneeling at
each station and making no genuflection and standing
at each station, or making a genuflection and standing, or kissing one's crucifix at each station, or saying
before meditating on each station: "We adore Thee,
O Christ, and we praise Thee, because by Thy holy
cross Thou hast redeemed the world," and after the
meditation, "I thank Thee, O Lord, for having died
on the cross to atone for my sins." (Both these prayers
are indulgenced.) The examples given are not exhaustive.

This manner of making the way of the cross, without a book, is perhaps the best way as far as real personal devotion is concerned. Recall that all that is
required in making the stations, in order to gain the
indulgences (one plenary indulgence each time, and a

second one the first time on Communion days, and ten years for each station if the way of the cross is begun and then for some reason cannot be completed, that is, for each station visited) is that you *move* from station to station and meditate at each one on the Passion of Christ. No vocal prayers are required and no prayers afterwards for the intentions of the Pope. It is necessary to move from station to station, so be careful not to take in two or more stations standing on the very same spot. It is necessary to meditate on the Passion of Christ, but you need not think of that particular phase of the Passion represented by the respective station, though that is what we naturally do, as a rule.

One can devoutly make the way of the cross in this way in five minutes or so, sometimes protracting the time, sometimes even shortening it and making up for the brevity by greater recollection and intensity. In the course of time you will feel that it is ever so much more prayerful and heartfelt when you make it in your own way, with your own thoughts and affections, than when you use a prayer book. But let everyone abound in his own sense. So many thoughts come to the mind as we accompany the Savior along the sorrowful way of the cross.

By the way, do not neglect to kneel down before the tabernacle before you begin the stations and make a little preparatory prayer; and when you have finished, make a brief prayer of thanksgiving.

An example of the many things to meditate on before the stations is the following, for the twelfth station.

JESUS DIES ON THE CROSS. It was some little distance from the place where Jesus was nailed to the cross, to the hole in the rock where they erected it. Maybe they turned the cross over in order to clinch the nails, as some say, and dragged Him along the stony ground that way. But it seems that the nails were not bent over. Then they hoisted it with ropes. They let it fall into the hole prepared for it. There was a dull thud. The whole weight of His body came down on the nails; every wound was torn open anew. Jesus twisted in agony, as much as He could, pushed down on His feet to relieve the pain in His hands, pulled down on His hands to relieve the pain in His feet, and finally hung still because it was no use. His thorn-crowned head hung forward. His eyes were filled wtih blood. His mouth was dry and His tongue black with thirst, and His lips blue and cracked. His bosom heaved. His muscles twitched. For three hours He hung there like that. If I had to stand in one position for three hours without moving, it would be an agony. If I had to kneel on one spot with my arms outstretched in the form of a cross, I do not think I could do it. I would die. As the hours passed slowly by, each minute like years and years, Jesus spoke His seven last words: "Father, forgive them, for they know not what they do." Jesus, I did not know that I was crucifying Thee when I sinned. "Amen I say to thee, this day thou shalt be with Me in paradise." So good is Jesus; for one "Lord, remember me" He at once promises paradise to a big sinner. "Woman, behold thy son; son, behold thy Mother." When thus speaking to St. John, He gave Mary, the Mother of Sorrows, to be my Mother also. "My God, My God, why hast Thou forsaken Me!" When I seem to be abandoned by everybody, even by God, I will remember this greatest pain of my dying Lord. "I thirst." When wounded soldiers are lying in pain on the battlefield, they do not so much cry that their wounds be taken care of as for water, water, water. Jesus died of thirst, too. But he thirsted still more for my love. "It is finished." It was all over now. He had finished the work He had come to do: my salvation, as far as He is concerned. The rest He must leave to my free will. He will give the grace. "Father, into Thy hands I commend My spirit." Then His head fell forward on His breast; He gave one last convulsive gasp, and was still. Jesus! Jesus! He does not answer. He is dead—dead on the cross for me. "I thank Thee, O Lord, for having died on the cross to atone for my sins."

What is this talk in some books about prayer not changing anything, that God has decided all things from all eternity?

It is not so easy to answer this in simple words. But suppose we put it like this. God is eternal. With Him there is no past, no future: all is present. All is present. That means that from all eternity God saw at a glance, if a first glance may be assumed, all things as they would happen in what we call time and eternity. In that glance He saw when and how He would make creatures. He saw everything that they would do. He saw that He would give them free will, that they would make use of their free will in such and such a manner, some for Him, others against Him. Present before Him were all the sins of men and all their repentance, all the evils brought into the world by sin, all the wars, famines, pestilences, earthquakes, floods, miseries, sickness, death. All was present to Him. We really should say *is* present, for with God there is no past and no future.

Very well, then. From all eternity He also saw the least little prayer that would be offered and the least good deed that anyone would do. And from all eternity He saw what sacrifices would be made for His sake. At the same time He saw which prayers He would hear and which He would not hear, because they would not be for the spiritual good of the petitioners. To be more concrete still, God saw that tomorrow you are going to call upon Him earnestly and urgently entreat Him; but it is not tomorrow that God is going to grant this prayer of yours: He granted it already in His eternity before you ever became man. Or because tomorrow's prayer will be foolish or lacking in earnestness, God will deny it; but not really tomorrow, for He denied it already in eternity. With God, Who has seen everything in that first eternal glance, everything is a foregone conclusion. Why pray, then, because He knows it all? He knows it because you pray; you do not pray because He knows it.

So prayer does not change anything, if this be understood aright. It does not change the divine disposition. It is part of the divine disposition and enters into the economy of creation from the beginning. Man, indeed, prays in time; but God, knowing all things, sees in His timeless eternity the prayers of all men and disposes all things according to the worth and intelligence of those prayers.

We may go ever further than that and say that, though prayer does not change God nor nature's laws, it does better than that: it shapes events, cooperates with God and nature in the production of things and events. What a grand conception of prayer!

What dignity, then, prayer gives to man on earth. He is a child of God, exercising his rights and privileges of sonship by cooperating with God in the fashioning of the world of men and of things, literally becoming a partner in the work of Divine Providence.

"We pray," says St. Thomas, "not that we may change the divine disposition, but that we may impetrate that which God has disposed to be fulfilled by our prayers, in other words, that by asking, men may deserve to receive that which Almighty God from eternity has disposed to give, as St. Gregory says" (*Summa*, 2, 2; q. 83, a. 2).

This should be a great incentive to rest peacefully in the arms of our heavenly Father and to pray with attention, humility, sense of dependence, ardent desire, and great perseverance.

Don't you think I have a right to complain if the ordinary confessor comes to hear confessions only every two weeks? The superior is very good about it and helpful and assures me that I may go to some other priest nearby who has the faculties. But I don't like to do that.

Canon 595 of Church law prescribes that the superiors shall see that all religious make their confessions once a week. As this regulation prescribes that the superiors are to see to it that the rule regarding weekly confession is observed, so it manifestly provides that the priest appointed must give an opportunity to the Sisters to make their confession once a week. If from time to time it should happen by way of exception that the ordinary confessor cannot come, no reasonable Sister would complain. An opportunity to go elsewhere would then ordinarily present itself, should one wish to do so. Otherwise one waits until the next week. But that should not happen often; still less should it be the rule that the ordinary confessor comes only once in two weeks, or less often, except it cannot be helped, as in mission territories where the priest comes for Mass only once a month, let us say.

Then the Sisters have to bear also with this missionary hardship.

Weekly confession is a great means of spiritual progress. High standards of religious life must by all means be maintained among Sisters. And a special obligation to lead them to the highest religious standards rests upon those priests who are specially delegated by the bishop to hear the confessions of Sisters. It is, therefore, a sad state of affairs when the ordinary confessor is available only at irregular intervals, or only when he is called.

Canons 520 and 525 strictly obligate the Ordinary to appoint an ordinary confessor for each house of religious women in his jurisdiction. This obligation is a grave one, to which corresponds an equally grave obligation properly to perform the duties of an ordinary confessor on the part of the priest appointed. The first duty of an ordinary confessor, of course, is regularly to present himself each week, on a day and at an hour pre-arranged with the superior and convenient to all the religious, for hearing their confessions.

Yes, you have a right to complain in the case you mention. And your superior has the duty to see to it that the matter is remedied. Except in the extraordinary cases suggested above, it can generally be remedied. She has the bishop behind her when she takes steps to rectify abuses in this matter. There have been abuses in this matter. As one Ordinary wrote: "As there has been very much neglect on the part of confessors appointed in the past in the matter particularly of regularity, the Ordinary hereby admonishes confessors appointed for Sisters, faithfully and regularly to discharge their duties. In cases of grave neglect, he will proceed against them according to the manner established for cases of ecclesiastics who are grievously delinquent in the discharge of duties imposed on them by competent authority."

On the other hand, we would not be too particular as to whom we go to confession, when the ordinary confessor is not available.

When the constitutions read: "If, however, a Sister is lawfully prevented from being present for the recitation of the Office in common, she should substitute for the Office the rosary of five decades that is to be recited daily," does that mean that she does not have to say the Office privately when she can find time to do so?

That is what it means; and it is a good, sensible rule, one that takes into account how Sisters may sometimes be prevented by an excess of work from being present for the recitation of the Office in common and hence gives them a chance to rest a little and relax while saying the rosary.

There are some religious orders, both of men and women, and also some religious congregations, which are obliged by their constitutions to recite the Office in common. The Code of Canon Law prescribed that in these institutes, whether of men or women, the Office must be recited daily in common in every house in which there are at least four religious who are bound to choir, and even in those houses where there are fewer, if the constitutions so prescribe it. This obligation is incumbent on the community as such, not on the religious as individuals, and is certainly fulfilled if four religious are present, probably also if only two are present, or if the Office is recited by novices only. Unless they are in major orders or are explicitly obliged to do so by the constitutions, the professed who have only simple temporary vows are not bound to recite the Office privately; but the professed of solemn vows who have not been present in the choir are bound to recite the Office privately. (Canons 578, 610)

But what is said above does not really apply to those communities of religious who are bound by their constitutions to the recitation of the Little Office of the Blessed Virgin, even though it is to be recited in common. The obligation of reciting the Little Office in religious congregations arises entirely from the constitutions, which have to be consulted as to whether the private recitation is prescribed for those who cannot be present when it is said in common. Generally it is stated that the Little Office shall be recited daily in common. If that is all, then there is no obligation to recite it privately; and it is the superior's duty to see to it that it be recited in common. Moreover, the obligation to recite it in common, even if expressly prescribed by the constitutions, does not bind under pain of sin; and, of course, the private recitation is not so binding either. The religious who has been excused from the common recitation of the Little Office, or who has been unable to attend for some reason or other, has no obligation whatsoever to say it, unless the constitutions so prescribe; and even if they do so prescribe, they do not bind under pain of any sin.

Unless the constitutions prescribe that the Little Office be said in Latin, it may be recited in the vernacular, that is, in any language. And even if the Latin is prescribed for the recitation in common, religious who have been absent and who are obliged by the constitutions then to say privately the parts missed may say them in the vernacular, unless the constitutions also prescribe that even such private recitation must be Latin. Usually the constitutions are concerned only with recitation in common.

Do you think it is really necessary that each Sister has her own place in the chapel and even goes to receive Communion in order of office, or age, or profession, or whatever it may be?

There are certain inconveniences when such a rigid order is observed. Again and again a Sister comes in, goes to a certain pew, then causes quite a commotion while she walks in one or more places—on the kneeler, obviously, in front of the other Sisters. The long-suffering Sisters then lean back patiently and make way for the intruder as graciously as possible—which, considering the moods and tempers of individuals, is not always *very* gracious.

They must get to their respective places so that the order in which they file up to the Communion rail remains intact. At least that is the situation which prevails in many convents. We think it could and should be remedied. Mother Church wishes every one to have perfect liberty of conscience in approaching Communion. One may go daily; indeed, one is exhorted to go daily; but there may be no compulsion. The superior by word and action is to let her subjects know that, though she rejoices when they communicate frequently, she sees no reason for reproof in the fact that someone occasionally refrains from communicating. There should be no rigid and quasi-military order in coming up to receive Communion. Where there is such order, there may sometimes be indirect compulsion, inasmuch as a Sister who really would not want to receive finds that her abstention would be a cause of wonder, because all too noticeable.

How could this be remedied? Some religious communities have long ago abandoned the practice of going to Communion in a definite order. The Sisters go up to the rail when, and in whatever order, they wish, as the faithful do in a parish church. Best thing, perhaps, is the cultivation of a mental attitude which gives everyone liberty of spirit in abstaining from Holy Communion.

Those who assist the sick, sanctify the dying, console the afflicted, know that they are doing to Jesus what they are doing to these suffering ones of His. My work is such that I can do none of these things. I feel a bit bad about it. What should I do?

It is very true that when we take care of the sick we are taking care of the Savior Himself. He said: "Amen I say to you, as long as you did it for one of these, the least of my brethren, you did it for me" (Matt. 25:40). He will say to those on His right hand, "Come, blessed of my Father, take possession of the kingdom prepared for you from the foundation of the world; for I was hungry and you gave me to eat; I was thirsty and you gave me to drink; I was a stranger and you took me in; sick and you visited me; I was in prison and you came to me." Then He assures them, when they express their astonishment, that they have done all those things for Him. Therefore they are blessed by the Father, belong to that Father who, in His eternal decree, had foreknown His own and prepared for their happiness. Their reward is so great because the King Himself had been by them fed, harbored, clothed, visited in sickness and in captivity. Thus the Son of Man identifies Himself with the cause of all men whom, as the Servant of God, He purchased by His death. Christian disciples could not doubt that they had done these things for the love of Christ; but even they could hardly have realized, without our Lord's assurance, that these were favors personal to Him, even if the visible objects of those favors were often their own enemies and perhaps His.

But that list was not meant to be exhaustive. There are the corporal works of mercy: to feed the hungry; to give drink to the thirsty; to clothe the naked; to visit the imprisoned; to shelter the homeless; to visit the sick; to bury the dead. And there are the spiritual works of mercy: to admonish the sinner; to instruct the ignorant; to counsel the doubtful; to comfort the sorrowful; to bear wrongs patiently; to forgive all injuries; to pray for the living and the dead. These are only the chief works of mercy.

Take for a moment the last good work mentioned: to pray for the living and the dead. In addition to others that you can perform, you certainly can do this. St. Ambrose says: "The Lord considers as done to Himself what we do for the suffering souls in purgatory." And St. Bridget says: "If by our help a soul is freed from the pains of purgatory, Jesus accepts this as if we had freed Himself and He will reward us in due time as if we had helped Him." That is but repeating partially what the Savior Himself said, as we read in the twenty-fifth chapter of the Gospel according to St. Matthew.

Therefore, you need not feel the least little bit bad about the fact that you cannot do certain specified works of mercy. As we tell in detail in our ten-cent pamphlet, *The Church Suffering,* you can help the poor souls, and hence do something for Jesus Himself, by Holy Mass, by prayers of all kinds, by the gaining of indulgences, by the heroic act in favor of the souls in purgatory. Esteem indulgences highly, as Canon Law says the faithful should do. Gain a number of plenary indulgences for them every day and also many partial indulgences.

In the retreat you gave us you said that if we would perform all the prescribed spiritual exercises every day, during the whole time prescribed, and with the greatest possible devotion, we would become saints. I'm trying hard now. I wonder how I'm doing. Could you give me some examination questions?

Very well, here are the questions for the examination, taken from our manual for recollection day. But you will have to correct your own papers. Be strict—but also sensible.

Did you always prepare your points of meditation carefully?—Did you call them to mind before falling asleep and upon awaking in the morning?—Did you make your meditation according to the usual method, or according to that method which has proved to be the best for you, properly observing everything that should be observed?—Did you make the customary reflection after meditation and did you put any special thoughts and resolutions down in writing?—In what spirit and with what benefit did you do your spiritual reading?—Did you make your visits to the Blessed Sacrament devoutly?—What benefit did you derive from them?—Did you make spiritual communions?— Did you make the examination of conscience with care and attention, both the particular and the general examen?—Were you especially careful to make the act of contrition well?—And did you mark down the number in your particular examen?—Did you recite the Office with due devotion, respect, and attention?

—Have you a predilection for reciting it in common?—
Did you say the rosary, morning and evening prayers,
prayers before and after spiritual reading, before and
after meals, with devotion?—Did you assist at Holy
Mass with devotion and spiritual profit, uniting yourself with the Supreme and Eternal Priest Jesus Christ
and with His mystical body the Church, offering Him
and yourself together with Him, and letting yourself
be offered as a member of that same mystical body of
which Christ is the Head?—Were you mindful of the
two great parts of the Mass, the sacrificial oblation
and the sacrificial banquet, in which you offered to
the Divine Majesty a pure Host, a holy Host, an immaculate Host, the holy Bread of eternal life and the
Chalice of everlasting salvation, and then partook of
that same sacrifice by receiving the Body and Blood
of Christ in Holy Communion?—Did you bear in
mind that the best way of assisting at Mass is to receive Communion during Mass and that the best
preparation for Communion is the devout assistance
at Mass?—How about your preparations for Holy
Communion and thanksgivings afterwards, are they
fervent?—Did you often renew your good intention
during the day?—Did you often raise your heart to
God by means of aspirations or ejaculatory prayers?
—Did you go to confession every week and that on the
day appointed?—Did you have (perfect) contrition and
a firm purpose of amendment?—Was your accusation
sincere?—Or are your confessions becoming a matter
of routine?—Do you better yourself, at least as regards
one or the other defect?—Are the faults you are wont
to commit due to human frailty, weakness, forgetfulness, or do you commit them with sinful affection and
full deliberation?—Do you often renew your holy vows

privately?—Are you always glad and eager to perform your spiritual exercises?—Have you accustomed yourself to some certain method in the various spiritual exercises?—Do you assume a posture worthy of the presence of God when you pray?

X

MISCELLANEOUS

In recreation one of the Sisters once said jokingly: "Look out; don't strike me or you'll be excommunicated; I'm a religious, you know." Is one who strikes a cleric or a religious always excommunicated?

According to Canon 2343 excommunication reserved to the ordinary is incurred by whoever lays violent hands on the person of any cleric or religious (man or woman). This laying of violent hands includes striking, shoving, snatching things from, tearing the clothes, imprisoning, or otherwise detaining. It is not restricted to manual physical attack. The physical injury need not be grave; it suffices if the injury is a slight one physically, but a serious insult against the honor and respect due to such persons. Such things as mentioned would not *always* be a serious insult.

Children do not incur this censure before they have reached the age of puberty; hence, a grade school child who would strike a Sister in anger would not be excommunicated. Nor are those excommunicated who do not know that this is a reserved case. They are simply ignorant of the law and find out only after the deed has been done. A mortal sin must be committed, else there can be no excommunication; hence, it must be at one and the same time a grievous matter committed with sufficient reflection and full consent of the will. Hence a Sister who would lose her temper in an argument with another Sister and without thinking would slap her in the face, would not incur the excommunication. The injury contemplated here must be done knowingly and deliberately.

Furthermore, this excommunication would not be incurred if the person attacking were acting in self-defense or taking just revenge; wherefore a Sister would be perfectly justified by slapping such a privileged person in the face were he to dare make unlawful and sacrilegious advances.

To incur this censure, the injurious actions must be sacrilegious and gravely sinful not only exteriorly but also interiorly, if not by physical injury, then at least by injury to one's honor.

This excommunication is therefore not incurred if the striking is done for a good reason, in just self-defense, as we have already suggested, and with due moderation. Nor is it incurred when the striking is done for the sake of correction: as when a father or a teacher, either personally or through others, administers physical punishment to a cleric in minor orders; as when a Sister in charge of old or childish or mentally ill Sisters finds that she can control them or make them obey or behave themselves if she slaps them or spanks them, firmly yet charitably.

The excommunication is not incurred if one strikes a person who is a cleric or a religious not knowing that this is a cleric or a religious. And, we repeat, it is not incurred if it is done without grave fault, as when such a privileged person is struck without full advertence out of sudden anger, or if it is done in jest. (Cf. Noldin, *De Censuris*, pp. 80-83)

Best thing is to be very careful about "laying violent hands upon" religious. If you should really incur this excommunication, go to confession and tell the priest what you have done. He will see to it that you get absolution.

How should I tell my sins when I go to confession?

If you go to confession frequently, and this, for religious, is ordinarily every week, as canon law and the constitutions prescribe, you will have little difficulty in finding your sins. A good practice is to think of your confession when you arise in the morning of confession day, to reflect upon it from time to time as the day goes on, to breathe little prayers about it to God. Then, when the time comes, you will already be pretty well prepared, remotely, for the reception of this sacrament of peace. Make your immediate preparation then, paying particular attention to arousing deep sorrow for the sins you are going to confess and for those of the past that you are going to include; arrange the order of your accusation in your mind and fix upon what you are going to ask in the line of

spiritual guidance or the solving of personal problems.
Then tell your sins to the priest.

Tell your faults quite simply, and briefly, and sincerely, and sorrowfully, just as if you were kneeling at
the feet of Jesus, just as they are in your mind, just as
they appear to you, according to your own feeling
about them. He knows all about them already, but
He likes to have you tell Him yourself, just as a
mother likes to have a naughty child come and tear-
fully tell the wrong done and the sorrow felt. Then
she is so glad that she is almost ready not to be sorry
that the child did it. The loving Savior is like that—
and so quick, so willing, so eager to forgive. Kneel in
the confessional as if you were at the foot of the cross.
Be simple. Be humble. Never pose or try to be grand.
Do not think of the priest, but think of our Lord all
the time.

*What is the matter when, with external regularity
of religious life, there are found in the same persons
rivalries, dissensions, and such like faults?*

Even among the members of the same religious congregation there are to be found rivalries, dissensions,
calumnies, mutual scorn, recrimination. Some are em-
bittered at the least expression of disparagement. Sad
to say, there are some whose hearts are shut forever
because of some slight wrong that has been done them
or a wrong that they fancy has been done them.
Others there are whose wounded pride knows no
healing because of some correction administered or
some disapproving remark made. Yet others pose as
lovers of justice and truth, as indeed they are; but
they needlessly hurt the feelings of others. They interfere right and left. They are fond of nagging. They
judge rashly. They are the ones who look down in

the telling expression: "Two men looked out through prison bars: the one saw mud, the other stars."

But there they are, observing the order of the day with the rest of the community, going to chapel, approaching the altar rail. It seems that they forget that as the bread for transubstantiation is formed of many grains of wheat ground together to form one substance and as the distinct grains must sacrifice their individualism and submit to be fused, the one with the other, in a close union, so in Communion: the symbolism of the Lord's Supper demands that those who sit at it form one heart and one soul.

How true, as the *Imitation* says, that "every perfection in this life has some imperfection annexed to it."

What is the attitude to take when sufferings come to us from the hands of others, when, for instance, we are the objects of malevolence, jealousy, treachery, contempt, and abuse?

Do not justify yourself! Bear this sharp mortification. See the justice of God toward you working itself out in the injustice of the neighbor. St. Margaret Mary Alacoque says in one of her letters to Mother de Saumaise: "My greatest grief is to think that I am in the way, and this often makes me desire death. I even think it is my infidelities which cause all the calamities I see happening around me. And what makes me suffer still more is that I cannot avenge on myself the injuries committed against my divine Savior in the Blessed Sacrament of the Altar.—I earnestly wish to leave no means untried to completely efface myself from the minds of men, to bury myself, if I can, in oblivion and their contempt, which is all that is due to me."

With this great lover of the Sacred Heart "loaded

down with opprobrium," look upon yourself as an
abyss of imperfections and ignorance. Such an honest
attitude will detach you from creatures, deliver your
soul from disorderly affections, show you the vanity
of man's evaluations. The fortitude required here will
lead to "victory through flight," as St. Therese, the
Little Flower, calls it. Wrongly accused as a young
novice, she felt that her peace of soul would inevitably
be lost were she to attempt to justify herself. There
was no safety for her except through flight, she says.
"Thought was instantly translated into action," she
relates. "I fled, but my heart beat so violently that I
could not go far and had to sit on the stairs to calm
my emotion and to enjoy in peace the fruits of my
victory."

You want to do God's will and now you wonder
whether it is God's will that you should be in religion
where so many unreasonable things pop up, where
you find petty persecution, where your zeal for perfection is not appreciated, where your good will to do
all things well does not win universal approval.

So remember that God does not will the wrong and
injustice from which His servants suffer; but He does
will that His servants embrace the sufferings involved
and bear themselves virtuously in their sufferings.
What you find unbearable verifies the definition of
suffering precisely because it irks you, thwarts you,
offends against your sense of the fitness of things, and
proves devastating to your sensibility. Remember that
the sufferings that spring from diversity of tempera-
ment, the thoughtlessness and even perversity of those
with whom you are obliged to live in the constant
exercise of charity and forbearance, indeed everything
in your religious life because it is the religious life,
community life, is the will of God for you.

Does anyone go to heaven without going to purgatory?

It is no teaching of the Church that the usual goal for the ordinary good Catholic is purgatory, that by-passing purgatory is meant only for those who are obviously saints, and that for the ordinary person purgatory is an inevitable stop-over, no matter how good a Catholic he or she may have been. The Savior has given us the means whereby we can go straight to heaven after death, with no stop-over in purgatory. That means is extreme unction, the "Anointing unto Glory."

Many, many souls go directly to heaven after death because of the sacrament of Extreme Unction, received with the proper dispositions, for Extreme Unction was instituted to prepare the soul to go straight to heaven without any delay in purgatory. This is the teaching of all theologians. Noldin says: "This Sacrament is instituted as a proximate preparation and disposing of the soul, that it may enter heaven without delay." The same author also says: "This sacrament was instituted to remove whatever hinders the soul's entrance into heavenly glory" (Nos. 429, 430). Pruemmer (587) states: "Since Extreme Unction is the immediate preparation for heaven, it should remove whatever interferes with the soul's entrance into heaven." Father Joseph Kern, S.J., in his book on extreme unction says: "Extreme Unction is the perfect healing of the soul with a view to its immediate entry into glory." Lehmkuhl (n. 715) holds that "Extreme Unction disposes the soul and prepares it proximately for entrance into heaven." Suarez, speaking of the sacraments of penance and extreme unction (disp. 41), thinks that "if this Sacrament meets no obstacles, it takes away every evil from the soul that might in any way impede or retard its entrance to eternal glory." Albertus Magnus (IV, disp. ii, ad 1) believes that "Extreme Unction was instituted to remove the remains of sin in so far as they obstruct the immediate flight into heaven." St. Thomas (*Suppl.*, Q. xxix, ad 1) says: "This Sacrament immediately disposes man for glory." But why continue with citations? St. Agbert, Archbishop of York in the eighth century, tells us: "It is written that the soul of one who has received Extreme Unction is equally as pure as the soul of a child that dies immediately after Baptism."

But suppose that one had not the time to receive Extreme Unction. Many such no doubt also go directly to heaven. The renowned spiritual writer Blosius says: "One who at the moment of death makes an act of conformity to the will of God will not only be freed from hell but also from purgatory, no matter how many sins he has committed; for he who accepts death with perfect resignation acquires a merit which is similar to the merit of the holy martyrs, who willingly offered their lives to God for Jesus Christ." St. Gertrude used to say three hundred times a day: "My Jesus, not my will but Thine be done." Imitate her by saying instead the indulgenced prayer: "May the most just, most high and most lovable will of God be done in all things, may it be praised and exalted forever."

St. Theresa of Avila once saw a holy religious man go straight to heaven after death without going to purgatory. When in her wonder she asked why he was so favored, she was told it was because he kept all his rules, excelled in religious observance.

Why must I suffer?

To understand this great mystery, as Father Eiten, S.J., wrote in the September, 1944, *Review for Religious,* "we must go back to Calvary and there vividly witness the thoughts and affections passing through our Lord's mind and will. Our Lord with His human intelligence foresaw all the happenings of this world— good and bad. At that tragic time as He hung dying on the cross His mind cast a glance down the centuries and took special note of the good works and sufferings which the members of His Mystical Body would bear. What a consolation that all-embracing vision of our good works, sufferings, and acts of self-denial must have been to the Heart of Christ! Christ, then, our suffering Victim, took all these good works and sufferings of the loyal members of His Mystical Body along with His own and offered them as the *complete Victim of Calvary.* Thus the complete Victim of Calvary, the complete sacrifice of Calvary is Christ's sufferings plus *ours*—our sufferings with Christ's. Christ's sufferings win the prize of the redemption, while *ours* share in applying or administering that prize of His infinite merits either for saving souls or making good souls better." Thus we become as it were associates and co-helpers with Christ in the great work of the redemption. What a privilege! Our whole life should be such an identification with Christ in the great work of salvation, especially the sacrifice of all our daily duties well done and all our little sufferings well borne. We should be victim souls, so that we may "fill up those things that are wanting of the sufferings of Christ in our flesh, for His body, which is the Church" (Col. 1:24).

The victim soul says to God, as it were: "Have no

fear, Lord, about sending me sufferings, for I desire
them, I almost demand them, and Thou wilt gratify
my secret wishes by letting me have them." This must
be done with caution, however; and with more caution still and not without consultation should one
vow to become a victim. The Savior at this time has
need of generous victim souls. Most of us will do
better, however, to live in the spirit of victims, but
not to pray for sufferings. We will find enough of holy
abandonment to God in our daily lives; and it will be
humble, without the splendor that glorifies self-obla-
tion. And it will be prudent. Let us often offer ourselves for the intentions of victim souls of the Sacred
Heart: in reparation, for the conversion of sinners,
that the Lord may bless the labors of priests and religious throughout the world. We may also say the following prayer of St. Francis de Sales: "My God, I
want nothing in the world but Thee and Thy holy
will. I have the most ardent desire to increase in Thy
love and in all the virtues, and therefore I am determined to accomplish faithfully Thy signified will.
But with regard to everything that depends not on
me, but altogether on Thee, I put myself confidently
into Thy hands, and I hold myself in a state of simple
and filial expectation, ready to do whatsoever Thou
shalt ordain. I desire nothing, I ask nothing, I refuse
nothing. Suffering has no terrors for me, because
Thou wilt always proportion it to my weakness. All I
wish is to let Thee conduct me as Thou thinkest well,
and to submit with love to Thy good pleasure."

However, for souls who are still wondering what is
the answer to their particular query, we may say that
we wish it to be well understood that when the Holy
Spirit inspires a soul to offer herself as a victim, provided she acts with the permission and under the con-

trol of God's representatives and continues, above all, zealously to observe and be attentive to her daily duties, then there will be no deception, no temerity, but a divine call. Such a soul may expect terrible trials, but she may also expect God's help, and the merit to be gained therefrom.

What was it that St. Theresa of Spain said about a good religious going straight to heaven without any purgatory?

In her *Confessions,* ch. 38, St. Theresa of Avila writes (my translation): "A very devout man was seriously sick. Now, as I assisted at Holy Mass I saw that he had already died and was going up to heaven without purgatory. He died at the very hour that I saw him, as I afterwards learnt; and I wondered that he did not go to purgatory. Then I was given to understand that he had to thank the conscientious fulfilment of his religious duties for that; for the Church out of her rich treasury has applied special graces to those who faithfully observe the rules of the order— graces through which they remain free from the penances of purgatory. No doubt this information was given me for my instruction in order that I might realize that the religious state and the habit are not yet enough, but that only through a truly interior and exterior spiritual mode of life will we become partakers of so great a reward."

There are various other means of avoiding purgatory. To mention some of them again, we enumerate frequent confession; the gaining of indulgences; frequent Communion; Extreme Unction, which is the "anointing unto glory," the key of heaven; Mass celebrated for the living. Then there is the spirit of penance, which can be developed by every Christian

and above all by every religious by the constant remembrance of past sins and by flight from the occasions of sin. To these may be added the loving acceptance of an earthly purgatory and of death, the practice
of doing everything for the love of God, detachment
from earthly things.

*What do you think of true devotion to the Mother
of God as understood by St. Louis De Montfort?*

It is not a series of particular practices of devotion,
but a way of life. This way of life is a state of mind
and will and not merely a manifestation of devotion.
Devotion, properly speaking, is more comprehensive
than practices of devotion. Take a mother, for example, and her children. Her love for the children is
something permanent, not to be identified with any
particular sign of love. But it has various manifestations, such as the care she lavishes upon the children,
feeding them, dressing them, protecting them.

The true devotion with its total consecration to
Mary is not precisely an act of consecration but rather
a state of being entirely consecrated to her.

The Christian life is a life of union with God which
is effected or brought about through grace. Through
grace we share in His life, are made partakers of His
nature. In this union with God we are absolutely
dependent upon God. We cannot perform one single
supernatural action without His grace. "Without Me
you can do nothing," the Savior said. Grace is a free
gift of God. And our dependence upon God is absolute because we have no claim to grace.

Now this life of union with God and of strict dependence upon God is also one of strict dependence
upon our Blessed Lady. The Church teaches that God
is the author of grace. The Church also teaches that

no grace comes to us except through Mary, the media-
trix in the distribution of all grace. Pope Leo XIII in
his encyclical on the Rosary, *Octobri Mense,* has this
to say: "Nothing of the great treasury of grace which
the Lord has stored up comes to us except through
Mary, for such is the will of God." And Pope Pius X
in the encyclical *Ad Diem Illum* says the same thing:
"Through her all spiritual goods are communicated to
Christ's Mystical Body."

From what we have said, it follows that the Christian life is based on the practical recognition of our
dependence upon God and our Blessed Lady. And it
was just this that prompted St. Louis De Montfort to
propose his total consecration to Mary as the best, but
not the only way of acknowledging her dominion over
us. For that consecration is not merely a series of devotions to Mary, good as they all are, but a state of life,
a state of continual dependence upon her. We give
her all that we have and all that we are; we dedicate
ourselves entirely to her; we give her even our most
precious supernatural possessions: our merits to guard
and the value of our good actions to dispose of as she
sees fit.

We can, as we have seen, do nothing without Jesus
and Mary. Then why not consecrate ourselves in total
consecration to Mary, giving ourselves totally to Jesus
through His most sweet Mother. Why not do all
through Mary, by fusing our intentions with hers;
with Mary, by taking her as our model in everything;
in Mary, by striving to accept her sentiments and dispositions; and for Mary, by considering her as the
immediate purpose and end of all our actions.

"Who," asks St. Louis De Montfort, "will so advance as to make this devotion his habitual state? He
alone to whom the spirit of Jesus Christ shall have

revealed this secret, the faultlessly faithful soul whom He shall conduct there Himself."

Under what obligation is the Sister sacristan when the key of the tabernacle is left in the tabernacle door after Mass or late evening Benediction service?

The first thing to do in such a case would be humbly to ask the priest in charge what to do in case she finds that he has absent-mindedly left the key in the tabernacle door. That will remind him that he should do something about it himself, that he should not be so absorbed in his prayers as to forget to remove the key.

However, if the procedure mentioned has already been followed without any effect, or if it is not prudent to follow it at all, or if the priest is not around and will not be back until the next day, the sacristan may follow the advice given on page 29 of our book *Information for Sacristans:* "It is ordinarily quite proper and even a matter of duty for sacristans to remove the key from the tabernacle door in case it was forgotten. In this case it is well to make sure that the tabernacle is locked." One can make sure that it is locked by carefully trying the door. The door should not be opened, of course, but if in trying it gives the least little bit, one will know that it is not locked and will make sure that it is. Then remove the key and take it away.

The key is to be carefully guarded, as explained in the Instruction on the Careful Custody of the Most Blessed Eucharist (Sacred Congregation of the Sacraments, May 26, 1938).

As regards the rector of a church: "After these services the key should either be kept by the rector in his house or carried about on his person, with precautions against losing it, or it should be deposited in the sacristy, but in a secure and secret place to be locked with another key which the rector should keep as above stated." But "in case he goes away, he may and should give the charge to another priest for the duration of his absence. If he is keeping the key in the sacristy under another lock, he should give this second key to the sacristan for the time of his absence if the tabernacle key is likely to be needed—a practice which is manifestly confirmed by general usage. In the case of a parish church the key is to be kept by the pastor."

As regards convents: "The key should be kept in the sacristy so as to be at hand when needed; and when the sacred functions in the church are finished, and especially at night, it should be deposited in a safe, strong, and secret place, and locked with two keys, of which one should be kept by the Superioress of the community, either personally or through another, and the other by one of the nuns, for example, the sacristan, so that the concurrence of the two is necessary in order to open the place where the key is kept."

As regards seminaries, colleges, schools, hospitals, which have the faculty of keeping the Blessed Sacrament: "The tabernacle key is to be kept in each case by the rector or head of the institution, if he is a priest, otherwise by the spiritual director or chaplain who has charge of the regular celebration of Mass and of sacred functions, and he must take good care that it does not fall into other hands."

All those concerned are "strictly enjoined never to leave the tabernacle key on the altar table or in the lock of the tabernacle door, not even during the hours

when divine services are held at the altar of the
Blessed Sacrament."

*What is really the meaning of the words of St. Paul
(Col. 1:24): "I now rejoice in my sufferings for you,
and fill up those things that are wanting of the sufferings of Christ, in my flesh, for his body, which is the
church"?*

"Assuredly, the Passion of Christ, the Savior, was
all-sufficient and all-perfect of itself; but Christ, the
head of the mystical body, wishes to suffer not only in
His own Person, but in all His members as well. It is
in this sense that the sufferings of those who have
been incorporated into Christ complete and perfect
His sufferings. What a privilege to be thus associated
in Christ's redemptive work! And who among us
would refuse to suffer with Him for such an exalted
cause! United with the sufferings of Christ, our own
trials contribute to our own sanctification as well as
to the sanctification of all those for whom we offer
them. We are now in a position to understand better
why the Saints loved the cross. They loved it not for
its own sake, but for the sake of Christ Crucified, considering themselves blessed to be associated with Him
in His sorrows. They embraced the cross likewise for
the sake of souls bought at the price of His Precious
Blood, cooperating with Christ in their salvation by
freely and lovingly undertaking sacrifices in union
with Him.—But we must not conclude from this that
suffering alone unites us with Christ. In virtue of our
incorporation into Him, all our actions become the
actions of Christ, our Head. St. Paul puts it well: 'I
live, now not I; but Christ liveth in me' " (Gal. 2:20).
(Tanquerey, *Doctrine and Devotion*)

Accordingly, when we pray, when we perform any supernatural act, when we are meek and humble, when we suffer, He dwells in us; we dwell in Him; we are one.

What effect should meditation on the Passion of Christ have on the devout religious?

The effect of such meditation may be 1. compassion for Christ. It may be 2. a horror of sin because one's sins crucified Him. It may be 3. a great love for Jesus who loved us so much as to die for us. "He loved me and delivered Himself for me!" we cry out with St. Paul. It may be all three of these things.

But the greatest and most important fruit of this meditation on the Passion should be a realization that the cross is the symbol of the Christian way of living; that sacrifice was the lot of the Savior and must be the lot of the saved as well; that the cross is not only for Christ, but for the Christian as well; that it is a book for all men to read; that the Christian calling demands that each follower of Christ develop in himself that attitude of soul which was Christ's as expressed in the Passion; that "whosoever doth not carry his cross and come after Me cannot be My disciple."

The cross bridges the gap between religious regularity and real sanctity.

No wonder, then, that the word *cross* came to be used, by Christ Himself, and after Him by Christians of every age, as a synonym for trials and tribulations, by the patient endurance of which perfection is attained.

An observant religious will find crosses everywhere: the vows, the rules, the order of the day, community life, plus all kinds of trials and temptations. "Hail, O cross, my only hope!"

Nowadays we hear so much about theology for Sisters, and there are special courses offered. Don't you think Sisters are made spiritually and intellectually happy when they study theology?

Yes, of course. And as one Sister of average intelligence, whose excellent answers in classes of theology surprised her teacher, said: "It is remarkable how much, in spite of my natural stupidity, the Holy Spirit lets me understand."

Such a course in theology, as presented in the University of Notre Dame Bulletin, would be, for example, like this: First year: the one God and the Trinity; the Principles of Spiritual Theology; Biblical Theology. Second year: the Incarnation and Redemption of Christ; the Theological Virtues. Third year: the Mystical Body and the Sacramental Life; the Moral Virtues. Fourth year: the History of Spirituality; the Theology of the Religious Life and Vows. Fifth year: the Theology of the Mystical Life; Psychology and Spiritual Theology.

Certainly teaching Sisters should know enough theology to solve problems brought to them by pupils and others. It should not be necessary for a Sister to say in a shocked voice, when asked whether she explains the catechism to the children as she asks them the questions in the book: "Why, no, Father, I would never dare to do that; I do not know so much, that is, I am not sure of myself; I leave that to the priest." Not all questions call for answer by a trained physician of souls, which every priest is.

In his address given to 700 Mothers General and other Sisters in Rome, September 15, 1952, Pope Pius XII said, among other things; in "the formation of your Sisters for the work and the duty which is theirs . . . show no narrowness, but be broad of vision. Whether it be a matter of education, pedagogy, care of the sick, of artistic activity or something else, the Sister must have this feeling: my superior gives me a training which places me on a level of equality with my colleagues in the world. Give them also the possibility of keeping their professional capacities up-to-date."

But a theology course such as we have given as an example will be the privilege of a comparatively few, at least in the immediate future. The majority of Sisters, self-effaced, lowly, hidden-away, do not as yet take such courses. And for that very reason those who do must be most careful that they do not look down from a lofty height, superior and supercilious, upon the ordinary Sister, who has had nothing more than a very fine course in religion. St. Thomas teaches that humility is truth. But there is one truth that the learned in theological or other lore can easily forget, namely, that they know little enough and that they are of themselves and before God nothing, to which nothingness they have added sinfulness. It is said by some who seem to know, that those who have, for example, a Ph.D. do not always give the impression that Ph.D. in the case of religious should first of all stand for Poverty, Humility, Detachment. A religious who forgets that she is *first of all* a religious and *then* whatever else she may be, is going to be a disappointment to the Savior.

In the address mentioned above His Holiness also says: "Without doubt, it is true, as psychology holds, that the woman, vested with authority, does not succeed as easily as the man in dispensing exactly and balancing severity with kindness. All the more reason for cultivating your maternal affection."

*Will there be other creations in God's eternity?
Eternity is a long time, you know.*

This makes us think of the eternity of God. We
mount up: through the Church, the synagogue, patri-
archs, and the long lives of antediluvian fathers,
through creation of man, countless cycles of inorganic
matter for who knows how many millions of secular
ages, then through the kingdoms of angels, then the
silence that was before creation—and the Blessed Trinity! And as God always was, so He always will be; He
had no beginning, He will have no end. He is one
God in three Persons, the Father, the Son, and the
Holy Spirit. He is the essence of all perfection. He is
infinite, eternal and immutable, omnipresent and
immense, omniscient and all wise, holy, good, just,
merciful, long-suffering, faithful, and true. He is
Goodness Supreme and most worthy of all our love.

(Now make an act of perfect love of God. Say, "My
God, I love You because You are so good." When we
say this, we should really mean the first part of the
Our Father, that sublimest of prayers, which contains
all the elements of an act of pure love of God: "Our
Father who art in heaven, hallowed be Thy Name,
Thy kingdom come, Thy will be done on earth as it is
in heaven.")

Different creations may have been made; new creations may follow. As Father Faber expresses it: "Creation may pass from orb to orb through millions of
worlds, as the Divine Fingers may choose to press the
bright keys of His stupendous instrument. The world
whereon the Word was incarnate may be the spiritual
center of unnumbered systems of worlds. The Incarnation will have gathered its glorified family about its
Head."

The religious congregation to which I belong was founded, not in the United States, but in a foreign country. At first all its members were from that country. Now that the congregation is trying to get a good start in this country most of the members are from the land of its origin, speak that language, sing those hymns, observe various customs peculiar to the homeland. I, as an American girl and one of the first to join them here, find all this very hard. I cannot speak that language; though I try to learn it, I do not get very far, with all my other duties; and sometimes during prayer I feel such a repugnance to saying something I cannot understand or even listening to it. Of course, I realize that it was God's will that brought me here, since He could have given me an attraction to an American community. So I just say: "God wants it this way." Do you think I am taking the right attitude in this matter?

Yes, we think you have the right attitude in this matter. God evidently wants you to be among the first American girls to join this community. Others will come—and then still others, until in the course of time there will be one or more flourishing provinces composed mostly of Americans. This thing has been repeating itself for a couple of centuries or more. As with parishes, so too with religious communities: some have been French, or Spanish, or Italian, or German, or Polish, or what have you, in origin; but gradually they have adapted themselves to the country of their missionary choice, until today there is almost nothing left of the old language and the old ways but a grateful remembrance of the hardy pioneers who bravely started a great work in a strange country.

Those pioneers! The more we think about those who are with us no more and those who, as in your case, are with us still, the more we have to admire them. They left the fatherland and came to a foreign shore, just as missionaries nowadays leave from the United States and go to distant countries. It was for them the same sacrifice, generously made. As American members joined their respective communities, they tried to adapt themselves as best they could to the ways of the newcomers, wondering how far they should go and how fast they should move in their adaptation to the new circumstances without losing the primitive spirit of the order. The oldsters had to be very patient with the youngsters—and the youngsters very patient with the oldsters.

Yes, God wanted it that way with you. Gradually things will change. And the older you get, the more broad-minded and understanding you will be. The time will come, we venture to say, when you will feel a sort of heartache when that good old language disappears, and you never hear those dear songs, and those deeply Catholic customs vanish, and the wonderful spirit of the pioneers, who were tireless in their labors and endless in their prayers, is no more. What is sometimes so repugnant to you now will be a pleasant memory then. And as you think back, you will breathe a prayer that, while necessary adaptations go on and on, there will be no mitigation of the original spirit of the congregation.

We close with a reminder to superiors that it will be hard for them to get vocations in our day unless such a community as yours changes so fast and so radically that it will hurt the living pioneers. Things were different fifty years ago!

Why is it so hard to get American girls to enter a convent where they will probably be engaged in housework of some kind?

This is indeed a puzzle. Most American girls get married, of course. And, as Father Buckley so well expresses it, "there is in this world nothing more beautiful than marriage—except the renunciation of marriage for the love of Jesus." When the blissful wedding day is over, the young wife begins to do housekeeping, first for two; and when the babies come, for more. Every day there is cooking and cleaning and dusting and sweeping and the laundry and the sewing —household duties of many kinds. This goes on day after day, with what would be crushing routine, were it not made light and joyful by love for the dear ones and pride in the home. For a lifetime it may be said of such home-makers that "a woman's work is never done."

Isn't it passing strange that when these splendid American girls become brides of Christ they seem to shy away from household duties, cooking, baking, washing, sewing, and all the rest. Teaching, nursing, social work, yes, oh yes! But domestic science, no, oh no! What a life that must be to be a cook in a kitchen for a lifetime! The brides of Christ are forgetting that He said: "Whatsoever you do for these My brethren, you do for Me," and that these who represent Jesus are the members of the community, or the priests and students in the seminary, or the orphans in the orphanage, or whoever they may be. Love for Christ will make also that work light and joyful.

They are forgetting that the life of our Lady, Mary Immaculate assumed into heaven, was spent mostly in the ordinary housework enumerated above. Alas and alas! too many are forgetting our Lady of the Pots and Pans. Our Lady of the Pots and Pans, give us many Sisters who will want to do what you did!

But the kitchen is such a bleak place. Imagine spending one's whole life there! Is it so cheerless after all? With all the modern equipment, with its time-and-labor-saving devices, with its manifold conveniences and its white and shining cabinets, it is a most homelike place. Compare our kitchens with the little house in Nazareth of which Mary was the queen. There were no electric lights, no heating, no refrigerator, no plumbing. There was no chimney; the fire was near the door so that the smoke could go out. If the wind was not favorable, smoke would come into the room and tears into the eyes.

What did they eat? Look into the pantry. You see a number of earthen jars. There are black olives, cucumbers, other simple vegetables: perhaps an egg or two, goats' cheese, bread baked in loaves like pancakes—thin and large, perhaps mutton or veal and fresh fish from Lake Tiberias, nuts and fruits for dessert.

There was the occasional burning of fingers and breaking of dishes, visits from relatives and neighbors. Joseph's shop was outside in good weather, inside in the rainy season, from November to March.

We want to think of Mary, Queen, spending her life in domestic duties in Nazareth, where "the Child grew, and waxed strong, full of wisdom; and the grace of God was in Him" (Luke 2:40). Chadwick wrote:

> When Our Lord was a little new baby
> And lay on our Lady's knees,
> He heard the bees in the clover,
> He heard the winds in the trees.

He remembered making the clover
And setting the wind to blow;
He remembered putting the hum in the bees
And teaching the trees to grow.

I am just an ordinary housework Sister and I often envy the teaching Sisters here. In fact, I sometimes go so far as to think that they are the fine ladies around here, who do not have to put on the blue apron at all! What do you think?

Perhaps you do not realize how hard the poor teaching Sisters have it—and how nice you have it by comparison. Of the teaching Sister, Father Joseph F. Gallen, S.J., in the July, 1955, *Review for Religious,* writes, among other things:

"She is confronted daily with the exhausting task of six or seven hours of teaching young children, or extracurricular activities, preparation for classes, several hours of religious exercises, domestic duties in the convent, and sometimes of added parochial duties. She may have to attend classes for her own education on some afternoons and on Saturdays. Her Christmas vacation is frequently taken up in great part by a second retreat, and her Easter vacation is sometimes devoted to the annual retreat. In the summer she is faced by summer school for her own education, her annual retreat, and sometimes by catechetical schools. In such a regime we can seriously doubt that she is capable of being soundly educated by the extra classes during the year and the summer school. We can affirm with certainty that sufficient care is not being taken of her physical and mental health and that she is not being given the maternal government demanded by Pius XII. With equal certainty we can hold that her spiritual life is endangered. She is faced by an impossible life. Something has to break; and experience proves, at least usually, that the first thing to weaken in such circumstances is the spiritual life."

So thank God that you are just a cook Sister!

INDEX